dwell

dwell

*A Journal for Naming, Processing,
and Embracing Your Emotions*

DEVON LOFTUS

A TarcherPerigee Book

tarcherperigee

an imprint of Penguin Random House LLC
penguinrandomhouse.com

Most TarcherPerigee books are available at special quantity discounts for bulk purchase for sales promotions, premiums, fund-raising, and educational needs. Special books or book excerpts also can be created to fit specific needs. For details, write: SpecialMarkets@penguinrandomhouse.com.

Library of Congress Cataloging-in-Publication Data

Names: Loftus, Devon, author.
Title: Dwell: a journal for naming, processing, and embracing your emotions / Devon Loftus.
Description: New York: TarcherPerigee, an imprint of Penguin Random House LLC, [2023]
Identifiers: LCCN 2022033669 (print) | LCCN 2022033670 (ebook) |
ISBN 9780593421000 (trade paperback) | ISBN 9780593421017 (epub) |
Subjects: LCSH: Emotions.
Classification: LCC BF531.L59 2023 (print) | LCC BF531 (ebook) |
DDC 152.4—dc23/eng/20220725
LC record available at https://lccn.loc.gov/2022033669
LC ebook record available at https://lccn.loc.gov/2022033670

Printed in the United States of America
1st Printing

Book design by Laura K. Corless

To the human heart and to my parents
for forever reminding me of mine.

To Kit, my biggest teacher: I love you.

Contents

groovy • 111

spacious • 153

transcendent • 201

dwell

Welcome Home

What a wonderful gift it is to be human—with eyes to read, a hand to touch, and a heart to feel. As humans, we have all experienced emotions. Sometimes vast and humbling like a canyon. Sometimes loud and exhausting like a busy city street. Sometimes soft and tender like the light that peeks through the window at 4:30 p.m. on a spring day. Sometimes heavy and knee-buckling, painting life gray and bare. And sometimes an emotion is so sublime that it fills every cell in your body until all feels right in your skin and the world at large. How emotions arrive and spend time with us evolve as we do, but without missing a beat, there they are.

I was eighteen years old when I met Depression. At the time, I liked to think of him as barging in like a violent gust of air, leaving me cold and breathless. But the truth is, he had been quietly arriving all along. Leaving bread crumbs along the way, hinting in his insidious manner as the color drained from my face that he would soon make a home inside me.

The truth was, I didn't have the tools to notice him. He disguised himself as "a bad breakup" or "freshman-year blues." I don't recall when it was that he shared his real name with me, but I do remember that in that moment, I was no longer the same.

Before long, it was Lean Cuisine for dinner with not much else to eat the rest of the day. The thought of joining my friends in the dining hall was too much. I was too tired. I stared with wonder at the bottle of anti-depressants on my desk, desperate to know, if they were to all enter my bloodstream at once, would the pain stop?

It was shortly after this that I made the choice to live. For my family. For my friends. And, without realizing it at the time, for myself. It was through the process of therapy and the choice to meet the most tender parts of myself that I began to value my self-worth and work toward understanding myself. I learned what empowerment felt like in my gut and how to give myself compassion, or when I couldn't, how to at least give myself permission to feel.

Throughout the years of therapy that followed, as I sifted through my past, healing trauma and rewiring my thoughts to more supportive ones, there was a key component. I was consistently and sometimes subtly learning how to understand, accept, and live with my emotions. I was having conversations with them. They were sharing things with me—vulnerable things, hard things, beautiful things. And the more I conversed with the emotions I met, the better I understood myself. Soon, the question no longer became how I *should* feel, but how to feel more deeply without attaching judgment. For so long, I had shamed myself for feeling in big, bold ways. And for so long, I had been running from my life. If we don't learn to acknowledge our emotions, are we truly living?

The title of this book refers to the places inside of us that our emotions dwell. I have imagined this book as a space where you can be with your emotions and stay with yourself, even when it feels like you're being swallowed whole and the desire to push away is real and fervent. By personifying our emotions and approaching them as we would dear friends, sitting awhile and conversing, we can begin to approach them with curiosity and compassion. We can grow to understand them and, in turn, ourselves more deeply.

PERSONIFYING OUR EMOTIONS TO ACKNOWLEDGE AND PROCESS

The first emotion I ever personified was Discomfort. My husband and I had just flown from our home in California to the East Coast, where both our families lived. Besides the couple of bags we had packed, we were also carrying the tremendous weight of a recent kitchen fire in our apartment, a new marriage, and a three-month stay apart at our childhood homes while we prepared to build a tiny house back in the Bay Area. There was a lot of change—quick change at that—and it left me feeling ungrounded and emotional.

One of the first nights we arrived, I sat next to a roaring fireplace at my childhood home. Our English bulldog, Olive, was next to me fast asleep, and time slowed down just a little. It slowed down enough for me to feel the discomfort I was carrying and for me to create space to sit with my emotion to better understand what it was trying to tell me.

What I heard surprised me but also gave me relief. What I heard was a voice that didn't quite sound like mine but came from within. What I heard was someone *else* in need. And so the conversation between us began.

Discomfort was soft yet rugged. He was intimidating and intense, but at his core, he was tired. He was lonely. He wanted to be heard. The more I sat with him, the more I understood these parts of myself; and the more I understood these parts of myself, the easier it was to have compassion and eventually acceptance for them, like I would have for another human. He helped shine a light on what I needed to feel secure and held.

That night I walked away feeling not only lighter but seen. I remembered that I did this intuitively as a child—created worlds and used narrative reframing to process fear, pain, and trauma. In taking the time to acknowledge, feel, and converse with my emotion, I gave myself what we all want and need and often look for from others—belonging and validity. And because of that, it was immovable. It was integrative. And albeit sometimes incredibly challenging, it was always there for me to return to.

Throughout *Dwell*, we will meet our emotions at their homes or at places of their choosing in different landscapes all over the world. When we can imagine where these emotions live in a physical realm or in a tangible way, we can begin to think of our emotions as having homes inside us, instead of taking over our whole selves. They begin to feel like people; they need to be talked to in a certain way, worked with in a certain way, held and cared for. Like people, they have their own unique set of terms, and we therefore have our own unique way of processing each of them. We learn how to approach each emotion we have with curiosity instead of expectation. The emphasis is not so much on where the emotions live, but more so that they, like us, have a "home" and a life that we step into. This humanlike humbleness is what makes them approachable. And it's also what makes them special to us.

My hope is that the rather whimsical process of personifying your emotions will also allow you to step inside your own imagination and creativity, giving you better access to your emotions with less judgment. When we're deep in an emotion, we're accessing our limbic system, making it hard to access our neocortex, or our "logical" thinking brain. Choosing curiosity or creativity allows us to move from our "emotional brains" into our "logical brains," to choose words for our emotions and therefore create worlds in which they live. According to the Flourishing Center, which offers the world's leading certificate program in applied positive psychology: "Word choice matters. Words create worlds. The more words we have to express our emotions, the richer our internal world is."

Within this book, you'll find forty-eight emotions placed into five different "worlds," or categories. As mentioned previously, this book and process are not about viewing emotions as negative versus positive. These categories are my artistic take on different ways we feel our emotions: prickly, full-bodied, groovy, spacious, and transcendent. As with the nuanced beauty of emotions, there are hundreds of thousands of different places our emotions live, and where these emotions live in this book are completely subjective. I encourage you to create your own categories in which your emotions dwell.

Creating worlds in which we meet with our emotions also serves the purpose of reminding us that we are *visiting* them. There is an arrival and a departure, and the mentality that emotions ebb and flow—that, as Rilke says, "no feeling is final"—is imperative to well-being and to processing emotions without feeling stuck.

This organization style is also an ode to the Dalai Lama's "Atlas of Emotions," which was commissioned with the purpose of growing our awareness and understanding of our emotions, how they're triggered, what they feel like in our bodies, and how we respond. As His Holiness says, "To find the new world we needed a map, and in order for us to find a calm mind we need a map of our emotions."

Having a map of our emotions, which we are inspired to create on our own, helps ground us in the truth that we have the power to be aware of our thoughts and how they affect our feelings. It reminds us that our emotions are robust, full, beautiful aspects of ourselves, and they are not to be feared but, rather, engaged with and acknowledged, like the people who make up our communities and worlds.

So, bounce around, make it messy, move more quickly through some sections of this book than others, or move slowly through them all. Your emotions will guide the way, as they are a part of you.

And we are deserving of self-acceptance for the challenging, scary, messy, gorgeous, and incredible humanness that lives inside us all.

Trust in that, and the compass will always point home.

HOW TO USE THIS BOOK

Woven throughout *Dwell* are short essays in which I describe my own interactions with different emotions. I describe them as I would fellow human beings who embody various human characteristics, mannerisms, quirks, fears, and desires. In this book, I hope to acknowledge and celebrate that emotions are a human experience, and therefore this book is inclusive to and celebrates all pronouns, gender identities, races, and sexual orientations, which you'll see reflected within the essays. These essays are meant to act as seeds of inspiration for your own process.

After each set of essays are workbook pages, where you're guided through the process of personifying your own emotions. This process is one I intuitively created as a child and picked back up as an adult.

The workbook pages and this process are yours to make your own.

We'll move through four steps together—greeting, sitting, conversing, and saying goodbye with gratitude—each with its own set of journal prompts or creative writing exercises.

When it comes to the prompts, my goal is to create a universal skeleton for you to use the same questions for all your emotions, focusing on one emotion at a time. In true human experience, there are many times when more than one emotion is present. To start with, I find it most supportive to focus on one emotion at a time and work your way up to one big meeting (complete with tea or doughnuts or whatever it is your emotions bring) if your emotions call to you in that way.

My hope is that these pages feel reflective and fun. If not fun, curious. And above all else, I want them to be yours—however that looks and feels. Add questions, take some away. Trust yourself enough to know exactly what you need to explore. The workbook sections act as space on a page to discover your internal landscape with intrigue and compassion and to get to know the emotions that live inside you a bit more.

THE PROCESS

In naming our emotions, we give whatever it is we're feeling a name—anger, sadness, fear, discomfort. It's a salutation of sorts. "Hello, Joy. It's so nice you're here." Studies have shown that naming our emotions increases self-awareness and decreases miscommunication within social interactions. From here, we can express our feelings in a way that practices respect and empathy for both ourselves and others. As Brené Brown so aptly writes in her book *Atlas of the Heart*, "Language shows us that naming an experience doesn't give the experience more power, it gives *us* the power of understanding and meaning."

We know we're sitting with an emotion when we feel it take up space in the body, causing physical sensations such as an increased heart rate, perspiration, jitters, butterflies in the stomach, heaviness on the chest, weak legs, and more. These descriptors vary, as we all feel our emotions in different ways. My goal is to find neutrality and not categorize them as negative or positive—they simply are a characteristic of that emotion. Much like I smell my mom's favorite candle burning before I enter her home, I feel a slight nausea and a shortness of breath before I greet Anxiety—these are signposts of arrival. Sitting with our emotions is to acknowledge the feelings without assigning meaning or judgment, without needing to immediately act on them or push them away.

We never aim to rid, cast out, demean, minimize, or scold any emotion. Instead, the goal is to gather tools for processing our feelings while moving through them with awareness, compassion, and, when possible, celebration and acceptance. It's human nature to want to quickly move out of a space where challenging emotions dwell, but that's not always possible or beneficial. Sometimes, the most supportive and loving thing we can do is be there for ourselves and one another, however that looks.

In the "conversing" part of this process, the goal is to talk *to* our emotion, not *at* it. By remaining a witness, we can ask ourselves questions to better understand why this feeling is present. Is there an external threat or a self-inflicted criticism that's causing me to feel a certain way? Is a boundary of mine being dismissed, or have I put that boundary in place yet? Am I angry or just really hungry?

From here, we can begin to unravel the judgments we sometimes place on our emotions (or ourselves for feeling them) and see them for what they are. For example, if Sadness greets me one afternoon and I begin our conversation with "Dear, God. Why are you here again? I'm always sad. There's something wrong with me. I need to fix myself," then sadness is going to burst into tears right there in my kitchen (as am I). It is a lot harder for me to converse with my feelings when I come to the space with bias and disdain. Thanks to the negativity bias—a biological response that causes us to give greater meaning to negative experiences or thoughts than to positive or neutral ones—meeting our emotions sans judgment can be incredibly challenging. We hear these negative stories about ourselves and our emotions, and they can feel wildly intense and true. Our confirmation bias, which is the inclination to believe, accept, and interpret information that supports our beliefs and values, may confirm that these thoughts are true if we already believe them to be so. (Spoiler alert: Not all thoughts we think are true.) It confirms only what our negativity bias says about us—we absolutely are sad all the time, there absolutely is something wrong with us.

If I can treat sadness like I would a friend, I find myself wanting to ask it different questions. "I'm here to listen. What do you need? Why are you here? And if you're not sure why, how can I help you feel more at home until we figure it out together?"

This space allows us to process our emotions with more compassion and depth. Notice I didn't say it allows us to process them more quickly—that hasn't always been my experience, and I don't believe this kind of self-awareness or practice is linear. Sometimes, I need to meet the same emotion several times in one day. Sometimes, I'll stay with an emotion for months or years. Big, transformative changes that take place on a cellular level require me to patiently (and not so patiently) walk beside my emotions for longer periods of time.

When it comes to saying goodbye, it can feel anything but natural or simple. To be honest, I've always found the "saying goodbye" process to be challenging and most times vague. When I think I've left an emotion's home, I find myself right back there moments later. When I think I'll dwell there forever, I find months have passed and I haven't visited in the same fashion I previously did.

When I say our last step is to say goodbye with gratitude, what I mean is to make peace with what we're feeling and come back to a state of presence so that our next conversation with that emotion will be a deeper, more cathartic one. I find that giving myself (and what I feel) gratitude helps me come back to my body, which allows me to pause before my conversing becomes ruminating.

Now, when an emotion meets me, I listen. Sometimes, I still shake. Sometimes, I'm at ease. But I see them for what they are, and I understand that in this lifetime together, I have so much to learn from them. I deserve that. As do they. Our emotions and who we are as we feel them deserve acknowledgment and attention. That is our life-force in action.

A NOTE ON MY PERSPECTIVE

Before we dig in deeper, I want to be clear that the process laid out in this book is not prescriptive, and I am not a licensed psychologist, medical doctor, or health-care professional. The objective of this book is to encourage you to be creative and reflective. The lessons I've learned in my own journey and the way I interact with my feelings throughout this book are my very personal and artistic means of expressing common emotions—they cannot account for all the beautiful variations in how we humans experience our emotions. These variations can stem from our own very particular experiences, which may include mental illness, racial injustice, or the reverberating effects of emotional trauma. It would be performative and dangerous for me to write about experiences I haven't navigated firsthand or haven't received clinical training to help address. It must also be said that emotions can cause serious mental stress, and it is never my goal to invalidate or bypass an emotional experience by suggesting that there is a silver lining or lesson to receive from every experience. Navigating emotions is a nuanced business. Every person's experience can be entirely different, as can their process—something I invite and celebrate. This book focuses on better understanding our emotions using writing as a tool but is in no way dogmatic. My only hope is to help normalize the feeling of our emotions and to offer a space for readers to reflect. My biggest request is that you make every aspect of this book your own, in whatever way that looks.

LET'S BEGIN!

If you're here, which I'm so glad you are, you value what messages our emotions bring. And if you're unsure how worthy this sometimes long and arduous relationship with emotions is, you're willing to find out. You're curious about how to navigate that inner world that lives inside us all. And you're open to understanding yourself and your emotions better, which, if you ask me, is a very beautiful, courageous (and human) thing to do.

So, cheers to the full spectrum of human emotion. To an open heart. To permission to be alive and the mess that makes. Cheers to dedicating yourself to yourself.

And above all else, cheers to being human.

prickly

Thorny · Stuffy · Itchy

As humans, we've all experienced uncomfortable and challenging emotions, whether they meet us as the sun rises, in the middle of a work call, while connecting with family, or in the quiet of the night. Prickly emotions are feelings we tend to resist, judge, or sum up. They're uncomfortable to experience and undesirable by societal standards. But their prickliness has so much to teach us. They may not always be easy to navigate, but they lead to emotional sustenance, like how a cactus leads to water. What softness can we give ourselves when prickly emotions ask for our attention?

Doubt

Doubt loves to sew. She sews everything she can get her hands on, from curtains to dresses to decorative planters that show off her lively fern collection. She also loves her fern collection.

Walking into Doubt's house always feels like taking a step back in time. Mustard yellows and burnt oranges move across her living room, giving off the most mellow, groovy 1970s vibe.

The truth is, Doubt is a total hipster by today's standards. I once asked her if she knew what a hipster was, and she replied in her midwestern accent, "Oh yeah! It's like a cool, updated fanny pack. The new rave these days."

She can make me giggle, especially when I can see her for who she is—an endearing, clumsy soul who wears her glasses around her neck but still spends a lot of time scouring the house for them.

But endearing or not, there are times when resting at Doubt's home feels uneasy and leaves me feeling lethargic. Times when I overstay my welcome. Moments when even Doubt herself wonders why I'm still there.

Her tweed couch is a nesting ground for discomfort. Sewing needles bury themselves into the seat cushions like tiny worms avoiding the rain. Every now and then, one surfaces and pinches my skin, leaving me alarmed and frustrated.

I rip apart cushion covers on my hands and knees, searching madly for the tiny point that's caused me pain. Sometimes, the source of the pain is so hard to find, I give up. I sit on the floor with my back against the end of the couch and cry softly. If I can't figure out where my doubt comes from, can I move forward?

One day, I happened to catch Doubt watching me as I ran through this drill like I have so many times before.

As I put my head in my hands and scoured my mind for where that sewing needle could possibly be, I felt her sit down next to me. Her face softened in the golden sun, and she looked like the old soul that she is.

She didn't speak. Her breath was quiet. And as she removed her glasses from around her neck and handed them to me, she put a soft hand on my shoulder.

"These should help," she whispered with a smile before disappearing to her sewing room.

With Doubt's glasses around my neck, her tweed couch came alive, and those needles came into sight. It took me time, but soon I realized that those needles were buried by no other than myself. A needle would catch the thread of my sweater as I entered through her front door or find its way onto the saucer of my teacup, burying itself in the cushion I now sat on.

Doubt and her needles have a way of sneaking into my heart, but with her trusty glasses, my own compassion, and the realization that I subconsciously put them there in the first place, I can gently remove them. And like Doubt, I can use them to create something new.

I studied the needle while I caught my breath, placed it on the table, and sat back on the couch, admiring the calla lilies that sat tall in the glass vase on the coffee table in front of me.

A quick shift, a worthy search party, and Doubt had softened.

I've never looked at those sewing needles the same way again.

Overwhelm

can hear Overwhelm's feet on the pavement before they come into view. The subtle feeling of static electricity in the air arrives earlier than they do, like a foreboding aura. I always know they're coming when I have a headache.

"I don't have time to be inspired," I think, as I nurse an iced latte. I can never seem to finish my drinks, whether they're hot or cold. The same way I can't finish my thoughts.

Or my breath.

When Overwhelm comes into view, I grit my teeth. They're striking, with straight stark-black hair and plump bold-red lips. When they smile, their catlike hazel eyes sparkle and their dimples come out of hiding. They are intoxicating at times, the way too much perfume can make you feel sick.

Overwhelm grabs my hand and I roll my eyes. They talk about life in such a hurried tone that my chest feels tight, and I struggle to catch my breath. I can feel my veins tightening, closing in on themselves. "Oxygen is a luxury," I think to myself, "when I'm around them."

They notice my state of being and tug on my shoulders to stop my stride. We sit down on the stone ledge of an apartment building as I put my head in between my legs, my sweaty neck exposed to the elements.

"Breathe, breathe, breathe," they say, while taking deep breaths themself. They hunch over so their body is level with mine, concern on their face. I notice the obsidian rock around their neck. They catch my eye and smile.

"Obsidian is said to draw out mental stress and tension," they explain. "It supports growth through acceptance and exploration of the unknown, an opening of new horizons, if you will. Plus," they whisper, "I think it looks badass."

I laugh softly and feel a heaviness akin to layers of knit clothing fall to the street below me. I decide to tell Overwhelm about the claustrophobic space I'm in; how my head spins and my body fills with longing— longing to rest, or better yet, to feel safe *to* rest.

"I become someone I don't recognize," I say. "Someone who retreats, who snaps, who cowers. Like a caged animal. A gray, weary version of myself."

They nod while I speak, actively listening, absorbing each word with grace and respect. And when I'm done, they turn to me, gently hold my face in their hands, and ask the question I've been waiting for.

"So, what do you want to do about it?"

Time spent with Overwhelm can hurt like a sunburn that won't heal. They pick and gnaw. They disrupt the day. But they do it to show me my boundaries. They do it to strengthen my integrity. They are an uncomfortable benchmark of what is and isn't working for me.

The same hand that just cupped my face now waves in the air, and I realize I haven't answered them.

"Friend? Are you there?" they ask.

I am here.

And for the first time all day, I take a deep breath and stand still as the city whips around me.

Shame

notice my face is buried in my hands only when something brings me to. I lift up my head and smell a savory pie baking somewhere in the distance, notes of lemon and rosemary dissipating in the air. But everything also smells sour. There is a queasiness in my stomach and a deep sense of unease.

I'm at Shame's.

My visits with him are brief. Sometimes, I don't visit at all. I just walk by, trailing my pointer finger along his iron-railed fence. But there are times when I know I'm due for a proper visit with Shame, that sitting with him awhile is important to understanding myself on a deeper level. And although I know Shame to be respectful of my boundaries, sometimes I find it hard to respect my own boundaries when I enter his space.

Somehow, his space feels comfortable and familiar, but in an ominous way. Like in dreams when you're in a place you recognize and yet at the same time it's not a place you know at all. Something is off. A sliver to the left. A bit duller. And by the time you open your mouth to scream for help, your voice is lost. Your arms are heavy. You've stayed too long.

Shame has the same effect, so I keep our conversations to the point. His long gray hair is straight and lifeless, but I stay focused by scratching my nail along his leather couch. "Why am I here? What good do you have to offer me?" I ask. It's not the kindest question, but it's all I've got.

He winces and looks up with his deep brown eyes. "I am a messenger," he says, sighing. "How about you just sit here awhile and listen?"

When I do allow myself to sit with Shame, I learn so much about the stories that I cling to. Judgments I've made my own. Deep, deep, deep pain I don't want to feel anymore. And most of all, ways I want to be free.

Free to be myself, love myself, accept myself. Free to break with society's conditioning and constructs. Understanding Shame allows me to understand what Freedom means to me in her entirety. His bitterness makes her all the sweeter.

"Freedom," I whisper back to him, almost forgetting I'm still there, the smell of rosemary and lemon beginning to overcome the sourness in the air. A timer goes off, and Shame quickly stands up, brushes off his apron, and walks to the kitchen. His savory pie is ready. And I take that as my chance to leave.

Frustration

Tiny pebbles of silt whip my face and my body as I make my way to Frustration's place. I pull the collar of my jacket up over my mouth to protect me from the dust storm. I quickly put my sunglasses on and my hand out in front of me, only for it to be swallowed whole in a matter of seconds. There is nothing to do but wait it out. I know. I've been here before.

Sometimes, these storms feel like they go on for hours instead of minutes. The lack of clarity, of cohesion, of anything recognizable makes me want to scream. Oftentimes, I do. This vacuum of dust that holds me so steady feels like a soundproof room, and I yell into the air, knowing that no one can hear me. This is why Frustration lives in the desert—she likes the structured chaos.

Soon, the wall of grit softly dissipates, and I'm left with the sound of my heart pounding in my ears. I'm breathless, dirty, and disheveled. I'm like a wild animal who has run herself ragged until her haunches can no longer carry her. It's then that I notice the silhouette of Frustration.

She's standing in front of me, wearing a long white caftan. She has on dirty, clunky brown boots with two silver buckles and frayed laces. She saunters over, carefully removing the linen scarf that hangs loosely around her neck and uses it to shelter her face from the storm.

"Hey, woman," she says with a playful smile. "Welcome home."

Frustration's ranch is made from classic adobe blocks and feels cool upon entering. She feels like the eye in a storm; everything outside her leaves me feeling fried, scattered, and rough, but when I'm with her—when I listen—things simmer. The mix of soft blue and turquoise that decorates her space helps bring me back down, as does the cool glass of water she hands me. And as we make our way to the tawny-colored leather sofa, I spot her artwork, perfectly hung on the walls. Jagged lines, zigzags, and deep circles that have been colored over and over again. Charcoal and pastels in black, dark blues, and fiery oranges and reds dance in disorder. I laugh at the juxtaposition of her calm manner with her artwork and almost choke on my water.

Frustration is anything but quiet or kempt, for the dust storm rages on inside her. The difference is she embraces it. She channels it. She understands that from feeling through her fire comes a release, a coolness—like the blues and greens she adorns herself with.

Frustration understands that we create our own mirages. That to reach the water, we must walk through the desert. And that if we're thirsty, we better pour our own damn glass.

The two of us talk for a couple of hours about art and our moon signs. We laugh and dream, and when it's time, I finish my water and walk outside.

The air is cool now, the storm is gone. But somewhere in the distance, a linen scarf blows gently in the wind.

And for the time being, the dust settles in my bones.

Guilt

t was nighttime when I awoke. The clock read 3:23 a.m., and I felt sick. Nauseous and uneasy, like something was terribly wrong. Miss Clavel from *Madeline* jumped into my head—"something is not right"—and I smiled, but only for a moment. I saw the light from the TV and I knew she was here.

Guilt was in my home.

I shuffled out of bed while my partner lay next to me, oblivious to who sat outside, which made her visit all the worse. I carefully walked across the wood floor, trying not to make a sound. Who was I trying to kid? Guilt knew I was stirring. My ghostlike ambition wasn't fooling anyone.

Especially her.

I allowed my feet to fall a little heavier as I rounded the corner and saw her sitting there. She wore a cropped black hoodie, which her long, thick, and shiny black hair was tucked up into. Her legs were curled into her chest, her hand was in a bag of Kettle potato chips, and her focus was on the TV in front of her. That was, until she heard me. Then her blue eyes were fixated on mine.

And that sick feeling was back.

I sat down next to her, begrudgingly, and was met with an arm around my neck and a tight pull into the side of her body. Guilt, by nature, was actually quite soft and sweet—something that was usually lost on me—but I knew, deep down, it wasn't really her that I dreaded. It was what she made me see, made me own. It was the responsibility that I had refused, the lie I had told, the heart I had broken, or the kindness and respect I had failed to show.

It had taken me years to realize that sometimes it was I who called Guilt in. Sometimes, I summoned Guilt because I wasn't ready to see my own strength and worth. I didn't understand that having boundaries was something to feel proud of. Feeling guilt for betraying myself reminded me that it was.

I thought about this as we sat on my sofa together; the bright light from the screen jarring and jagged—like watching cartoons with a fever. And yet the more time that passed, the more I sat with Guilt, the more at peace I felt. I knew why she was here, why she came at all. I knew it was a pulse check on my values; a mirror to reflect back if I was showing up in life the way that I wanted to, in a way that felt aligned with who I am and who I'm becoming. And most of all, if I was treating myself and others with the love and respect we deserve.

I knew that at the end of the day or, in this case, the end of a long night, Guilt would show me compassion for both myself and anyone I'd hurt. She'd lead me to Forgiveness's forest home and sit me down next to Acceptance and her chocolate chip cookies. Guilt is a leader, I realized. An essential part of having empathy and a heart.

I put my legs up on the ottoman in front of me and leaned a little closer into her. She nestled her head into mine before sitting up and turning to look at me, the potato chip bag in her hands.

"Chip?" she asked with a smile.

And I nodded yes.

Rejection

The desert is eerily calm. A still, subtle energy. "Hold still," it says, "or risk being found."

The mood makes sense, really. I'm meeting Rejection, after all.

And he stings as much as the saguaro cactus that sits next to me.

But I stay. I know at this point that meeting Rejection doesn't always end in loss. So I pull my olive-green linen zip-up over my face to shield it from the sun and wait for Rejection to pull up in his 1940s Chevrolet pickup.

I can hear its steady hum a mile away.

Soon, his trusty soundtrack comes into earshot, and I sit up tall, waiting to greet him.

He closes the scarlet-colored door behind him and walks over to me. As he adjusts his Stetson hat adorned with a silver feather, he smiles at me and plays with the toothpick in his mouth. We glare at each other for a second, as though we're in a gunfight, seeing who will pull their gun first, and then break into laughter.

Rejection grabs my shoulders hard, pulls me in, and hugs me tightly.

I can feel the stubble from his face against my forehead, and I let go as my hands find his waist and squeeze tighter.

This is certainly not how all our greetings transpire. We've had our fair share of arguments, Rejection and I. There are some things in life I don't think it was fair for him to take away. There are some things I feel are mine. But Rejection is the most loyal person I have ever met. His wife is Opportunity, after all. And the two of them never work alone.

There have been moments when I've found myself lost in the desert after meeting Rejection. It's time to head home—the goose bumps on my skin alert me with each inch of fading light—but I can't go. I gnaw at hangnails. And whimper under moonlight. I mourn what I feel I have lost. But the morning always comes, and Rejection meets me with the early signs of life, reminding me that it continues on, that I can choose again.

In these moments, he offers me his hand and pulls me out of sandy dunes, then delivers a hot cup of tea and homemade cider doughnuts. It's enough to make me shake my head in frustration and humble me simultaneously.

This visit, he skips right to the end and hands me a beautiful vintage tea set.

"To make your own tea when you're ready," he says proudly.

Rejection knows me so well.

I raise the gold-rimmed teacup as if to say, "Tea?"

He shakes his head with a chuckle and says, "Naw, I'm not a big tea guy myself. But if you had lemonade, now that's a different story."

We sit on the desert floor and laugh for a bit. Rejection wipes his now dusty hands along his stubble and smiles softly. I give my thanks before standing up, brushing off my sandy jeans, and heading back to my car.

That's when I check my pocket for my keys and feel something soft and bristly.

I reach in, pull it out, and hop into my car.

"Always with the silver lining," I say out loud to myself as I put the silver feather from Rejection's hat on the dashboard.

I follow it the entire way home.

Disappointment

There's a sense of longing that comes with Disappointment. A yearning. A deep pain. Grief at the loss of something I once claimed as my own.

I have a hard time letting go of possibility and expectations; I know that's part of it. It's something that Disappointment points out to me every time I meet them—a meeting they're usually late for, like today. I roll my eyes and sigh.

On days when the sun hangs higher in the sky, I don't wait for Disappointment. I gather my belongings and head straight to Rage. It's a tricky road to walk, though, for I know Rage will only pour tequila on my already burning wounds. Sometimes, that feels good. But most days, I find the patience to sit on the cool sand and wait for Disappointment to arrive in their own time.

Eventually, I see them. They're wearing light-blue linen pants and a white T-shirt. Their eyes are dark and inviting. They walk with no urgency, which angers me even more. "We had an appointment," I think. "Why do they always do this?" But that thought is quickly transformed when they sit down next to me, apologize for being late, and look out over the dunes. What they lack in punctuality they make up for in charm.

We meet on the white sand they know and love so much. Disappointment tells me that this sand is formed from gypsum, a soft mineral left behind when bodies of water evaporate.

I watch them pick it up in their hands and filter it through their fingers carefully, as it falls back to the earth. I copy them, allowing the sand to run through my fingers over and over. Somehow, it begins to feel softer, and every grain of sand returns to its rightful place in a vast universe of white.

After a few moments, Disappointment runs their hand through their black hair; tiny grains get caught and give the illusion of dandruff. I smile.

"Can you imagine if this body of water didn't evaporate?" they say as they look up at me. "We wouldn't be here together. You wouldn't be who you are right now. I wouldn't have sand in my hair." They smile and wink. I nudge their shoulder and smile back.

"But the pain is so heavy at times," I reply. "My dreams get redirected. Sometimes, I feel forced to let go of my vision completely. It would be easier if you came on time. It would be easier if maybe you didn't come at all."

This hurts Disappointment—I can feel their body softly wince next to mine. But they stay in the conversation. "Would it, though?" they ask. "Would it be easier to have everything you want? When you want it? How you want it? And when it concerns others, is that even fair? What about growth, possibility, mystery? What about trust?"

I sit and think about this for a long time, even though my soul knows the answer immediately. The truth is that Disappointment shows me my dreams, my needs, and my desires. They are a barometer on my ability to self-govern my world and choose myself. Every time I feel them underneath my skin, something is apparent: I want something and I'm not prioritizing it; I need something and I'm not voicing it, or my expectations need attention and a healthy gut check. I'm forgetting my sovereignty. I'm forgetting to surrender.

Within every opportunity or unmet expectation is another chance to evolve.

Disappointment reminds me that if bodies of water can do it, my body can, too.

I look back up at them and grasp their hand gently. Our time comes to an end when the sun sets. I'm grateful for their wisdom, for the possibilities that lie ahead, and for the keeper of time that they are.

And for the soft sand that made the choice to hold my body all those years ago in a different form, so I could exist in this one.

Judgment

J udgment is sentimental, though she'd never admit it. She may hint at it, she may even reveal a vulnerable side when her guard is down, but she'll never admit she has an aching to belong like the rest of us.

In the beginning, this was fine by me. First impressions leave a taste in my mouth, and Judgment tasted like cheap vodka and cigarettes. I avoided her. I scoffed at her. I judged her right back, unable to see the wounded child and loneliness that filled her.

But one night, a few years back, all of that changed.

Judgment and I found ourselves in a smoky bar on a Saturday night. It was the dive kind, where stale beer can be found on sticky bar stools and on the soles of your shoes. There was a comfort here; a feeling hung in the air and let you know you were welcome just as you are. This was Judgment's favorite place. These were Judgment's favorite people.

I spent time talking with the bartender, playing with the buttons on my coat, when a couple of men walked over and started talking with us.

I watched as Judgment pulled the collar of her black leather jacket closer to her porcelain skin. She smelled like crushed black pepper mixed with vanilla. This was her signature scent.

A man with long, wavy dirty-blond hair and piercing eyes showed a genuine interest in Judgment. He asked her question after question and stared deeply into her green eyes with a longing to understand her. To him, it may as well have been just the two of them in the room. She gazed back, meeting his every inquiry, both of them sinking deeper into intimacy while the bar chaos spun on around them.

Eventually, it was closing time. The bar lights dimmed, and beer glasses clanked their way to the bartender—a soon-to-be bedtime for ale-soaked objects and ale-soaked humans. When it came time to say goodbye to her admirer, Judgment's body language changed. Her leather jacket was now completely zipped up. Her hands were in her pockets. Her eyes were on the wall behind him. She looked over at me, nodded toward the bathroom, and walked away. I followed.

Judgment was standing over the sink with her face in her hands and her leather jacket over one shoulder. She continually brought cool water up to her lips and skin before slumping to the ground, her sweaty back against the cool tile. We sat on that dirty bar floor for ten minutes with nothing but the sound of a leaky faucet and the muffled sobs of Judgment.

When we returned to her apartment, she sat on the couch with a glass of whiskey in her hand. She didn't say anything—she allowed the air to fill with the smell of alcohol and my own thoughts.

"It's hard to feel seen sometimes," she said, pausing to take another sip, "and not worry that I'm not enough."

I slowly nodded. I knew what she meant, how that felt. I had found myself at Judgment's quaint Craftsman home often, criticizing myself or someone else. The could-haves, would-haves, should-haves swirling around my head like witches in ritualistic dance while Judgment turned up the music and poured me more whiskey.

Now it was my time to give her what I always needed when I arrived here. Love. Acceptance. The permission to be human.

I got up, sat down next to her, took the glass from her hand, and stared her in the eyes.

"You are imperfect, flawed, and wounded. That's what makes you human. That's what makes you alive. For everything you are and everything you aren't, you are loved."

Water welled in the corners of her eyes, and she looked down for a moment before looking up and laughing.

"Oh, and *I'm* the sentimental one," she said with a smile before pulling me in and holding me close.

We continued the rest of the night with whiskey cocktails, French house music, and homemade fries. And when the sun began to rise in the morning, I gathered my things and turned to leave.

"Wait," she said softly as she rubbed her eyes and slowly stood up to pick something off the table. It was her leather jacket, and she handed it to me to wear. I smiled and grabbed it, pulled it on, and smelled the mix of black pepper and vanilla.

I held it close to my skin as I walked the quiet streets back home.

Uncertainty

The waiting game is hard.

The waiting game takes everything I have and more.

Uncertainty leaves me bare-boned and scared like a child longing for a parent who feels a world away.

My body tries to flee, but it's too hot to move. The sun feels unbearable, like it's stretching, reaching closer to the ground, trying to touch me. I resemble clay that's being fired too quickly; rigid and fractured.

I cry out for help, wondering where in the atmosphere my cries will land. In the clouds? In gusts of wind? How will anyone find me here?

But in that moment, Uncertainty and Possibility arrive and run me inside, my call still echoing off the sky above us.

They sit me down on the cool kitchen tile, wrap me in a linen sheet, and stroke my hair. They take an icy washcloth from the freezer, place it on my forehead, and hold me.

Tightly.

My crying quiets, and Uncertainty wipes tears from my face. He smiles.

"You're safe in the waiting," he whispers. "You're safe. You're safe. You're safe."

And I remember that I am.

The memories rush back; my life happening in the uncertainty of it all. Every day with every breath, my life lives. I move and greet and bellow and cackle. I rage and cry and laugh so hard, the clouds part to make space. My life unfolds in the unknown. I live harmoniously with Uncertainty.

Possibility takes my hand now and leads me to the surprisingly comfortable couches in Uncertainty's living room. She reminds me of the power that Uncertainty hands me. The power to be present. The power to love deeply; here and now. The power of gratitude, of joy, of resilience. The power to show up, love up, clean up, and come home no matter the weather.

The gift of Uncertainty is to be certain of myself despite it all. The gift of Uncertainty is to be alive.

I sit up a little taller and stretch my arms overhead. My skin is cool. My heart is calm.

The waiting game continues, but this time I have Uncertainty and Possibility in my corner.

Asleep on the couch, hand in hand.

And I live on.

Discomfort

Last night I sat with Discomfort. I poured him a glass of Scotch, sat cross-legged at his feet, and listened to him tell tales of his great-grandfather and how he'd ruled with a heavy hand. "Never budge," his grandfather would say. "Always stay firm and wound tight. Resting is for the lazy."

I slowly shook my head as if to say that I felt for Discomfort. He looked down at me, quickly avoiding eye contact, and cleared his throat. "So," he continued, "I never really learned to sit with myself."

I knew this feeling, of sitting with Discomfort. I was doing it now, but it had taken me years to get here. Some days, still, when Discomfort walks in with a lit cigar in his rough hands, I cower. But then I remember that he, too, needs company. And so I sit.

As the night went on, and the embers created a halo effect in the fire, I realized that Discomfort had softened. Where a stern face used to rest was a jovial old man—his coarse laugh was so deep that it turned into a cough that echoed off the cabin walls. It was here that I caught a glimpse of his blue eyes.

I stood up, said my goodbyes, and walked home.

How strange, I thought, to meet the man behind the wiggles, the "get me out of here" sensation, and the "this sucks" mentality.

And yet all I could think about as I walked past tall trees and winds that kissed my cheeks were those gorgeous blue eyes.

A LITTLE BIT ABOUT THE WORKBOOK PAGES

Welcome to your process. These prompts and exercises, which you'll find at the end of each section, are organized into four steps: greeting, sitting, conversing, and saying goodbye with gratitude. This is the place you can come to when an emotion makes itself known and you'd like to explore what it has to say.

This space is entirely yours to fill in, leave blank, take time to ponder, use as inspiration, answer further in a notebook, create your own prompts, or come back to when you're ready. It's a space to reflect, to foster curiosity and compassion, and to get to know the places inside you a bit more.

Workbook Pages for
prickly

STEP 1: GREET

You feel an emotion is present. Say hello and acknowledge that it's here while doing your best not to attach judgment or try to change it, fix it, or remove it. Let it take up space. You can do this. Your body can hold it all.

Now, you can name it. Hello, ... Welcome.

In my body

You feel like . . .

. . . .

. . . .

. . . .

. . . .

. . . .

You taste like . . .

....

....

....

....

....

....

You smell like . . .

....

....

....

....

....

....

You make me want to . . .

....

....

....

....

....

....

....

As a messenger

You teach me . . .

....
....
....
....
....
....

You show me . . .

....
....
....
....
....
....

You need this to feel seen and heard . . .

....
....
....
....
....
....

Your secret is . . .

....

....

....

....

....

....

....

IF YOU NEED A RAINCHECK:

You need me to make space for you right now, but I don't have the time, accessibility, or availability at the moment. I have a sweet little sun-filled room where you can sit and wait. I'll be back. In the meantime, know that I see you and I'm here to listen.

Time I'll be back:

....

....

....

....

....

....

....

STEP 2: SIT

Hi, it's me. I'm here and ready to sit down to get to know you better. I know you have messages to share and ways to help me grow and heal. Let's sit together and discover the reason for your visit.

What activating event (an experience or a trigger) has currently introduced me to this emotion?

. . . .

. . . .

. . . .

. . . .

. . . .

. . . .

Right after the activating event and before I found myself with this emotion, there's a voice. This can be a belief or a story—something we tell ourselves either out of conditioning or previous experiences. What does this voice or this story say?

. . . .

. . . .

. . . .

. . . .

. . . .

. . . .

How does this story make me feel?

. . . .

. . . .

. . . .

. . . .

. . . .

. . . .

. . . .

. . . .

. . . .

And how does this emotion cause me to react?

. . . .

. . . .

. . . .

. . . .

. . . .

. . . .

. . . .

. . . .

. . . .

How can I honor exactly how I feel? How can I respect what I need most
in this moment?

. . . .

. . . .

. . . .

. . . .

. . . .

. . . .

. . . .

. . . .

What is one thing I can do for myself while I'm feeling this emotion that
will bring me nourishment? What feels safe here?

. . . .

. . . .

. . . .

. . . .

. . . .

. . . .

. . . .

. . . .

. . . .

STEP 3: CONVERSE

I'm glad we decided to sit down. It may not have been easy or simple, but it created space to understand each other better. It's time for a heart-to-heart.

Let's personify my emotion by cuing into my senses. Is it cold or warm? Does a breeze blow, or is it humid and thick? What do I feel on my skin when I close my eyes? What do I taste in the air? What smells draw me in? What colors stand out to me?

Where is our meeting place? Am I at my emotion's home, or do we meet somewhere else? Describe the landscape.

....

....

....

....

....

....

....

....

....

What does their home look like? Is their front door ornate or plain? Explain the exterior of their home and what surrounds it.

....

....

....

....

....

....

....

....

....

....

When I step inside their house, what textures do I find? What aesthetic themes emerge? Does it feel warm and cozy or minimalistic and drab? Is there food cooking or the scent of flowers on the table? What stands out to me about stepping into their world?

....

....

....

....

....

....

....

....

When I see the emotion, what does he/she/they look like? What feels striking about them?

....

....

....

....

....

....

....

....

....

What is their disposition? Are they kind? Jovial? Rugged? Quiet?

. . . .

. . . .

. . . .

. . . .

. . . .

. . . .

. . . .

. . . .

. . . .

Do they have a hobby? What do they love to do? What makes them come alive?

. . . .

. . . .

. . . .

. . . .

. . . .

. . . .

. . . .

. . . .

. . . .

What hurts them, scares them, worries them?

What about them surprises me? Speak to their duality.

What stories do they share? What past lives do I learn about? What do they need me to know? Write some dialogue.

. . . .

. . . .

. . . .

. . . .

. . . .

. . . .

. . . .

. . . .

. . . .

What is one element about our time together that feels important or stands out?

. . . .

. . . .

. . . .

. . . .

. . . .

. . . .

. . . .

. . . .

Is there a shifted perspective and/or physical item(s) I walk away with that reminds me of our time together?

. . . .

. . . .

. . . .

. . . .

. . . .

. . . .

. . . .

. . . .

. . . .

What is this emotion here to tell me?

. . . .

. . . .

. . . .

. . . .

. . . .

. . . .

. . . .

. . . .

. . . .

. . . .

What is one thing I can do right now to help myself and this emotion feel more loved, seen, and accepted?

STEP 4: GRATITUDE AND GOODBYE

I am so grateful for you because you are a part of me. And I am so grateful for me because I am here—growing, committing, and recommitting, messy and disheveled and present. I am a human, and for that I applaud myself. This is my thank-you letter to my emotion and to myself. I acknowledge us for who we are as fully as I can—always holding the easy, the hard, and everything in between.

What insight(s) did I uncover that I'd like to thank my emotion for leading me to?

. . . .

. . . .

. . . .

. . . .

. . . .

. . . .

. . . .

. . . .

. . . .

. . . .

. . . .

. . . .

. . . .

What part of my emotion and myself am I able to shed a softer light on?

....

....

....

....

....

....

....

....

....

What newfound gratitude do I have for myself and my emotion?

....

....

....

....

....

....

....

....

....

What story was I able to reframe about this emotion?

. . . .

. . . .

. . . .

. . . .

. . . .

. . . .

. . . .

. . . .

How does this new thought/perspective make me feel?

. . . .

. . . .

. . . .

. . . .

. . . .

. . . .

. . . .

. . . .

When I process this emotion, what other supportive emotions do I have access to?

How has this process shifted the way I react/respond to feeling this emotion, whether toward myself or toward someone else?

For many of us, the relationship we have with emotions is complex. We are often taught that feeling our emotions is inconvenient and unproductive; they slow us down, hang us up, stop us on our "climb to the top." We're told to "get over it," to "stop being so sensitive," or to "play it cool." Sometimes, we're taught to hide, cower, or deny altogether. Many of us have been conditioned at a young age to pass judgment on our emotions on the basis of how comfortable or uncomfortable they make others, turning feeling into the likes of a dating app—swipe left for grief, and right for joy.

So, why do we want to feel our feelings in the first place when, historically, society believes that being vulnerable, raw, and messy with what we feel (unless done within logical reason) can be shameful, weak, and embarrassing?

And since studies have shown that belonging is a basic primal need of ours and directly tied to our well-being and social motivation (stemming from the time we are born), why would we dare venture out and not only acknowledge our feelings but also get to know them

and embrace them? Or, hardest of all, share them with others? Why is choosing to foster emotional intelligence a worthy endeavor when it's often met with challenge, discomfort, and a deep sense of navigating a foreign land?

This is a very real question, and there is no right or wrong answer—a prominent theme in this book and this process. There is only *your* answer, and that's what makes this process so powerful. But there is one truth that will forever ring loudly: If we don't address our emotions, they will fester. Our intense, loud, powerful emotions will grow inside us like a hungry jungle, eventually ravaging everything we touch, the relationships we hold, and the life we lead. As Marc Brackett, author of *Permission to Feel: Unlocking the Power of Emotions to Help Our Kids, Ourselves, and Our Society Thrive,* puts it, "Hurt feelings don't vanish on their own. They don't heal themselves. If we don't express our emotions, they pile up like a debt that will eventually come due."

We base most of our decisions in life on how they make us feel, for better or worse. Without the tools to communicate with our emotions, we may feel unsure in our decisions altogether. Take happiness, for instance. If we don't engage with our joy and what creates it, we may chase unaligned careers, unaligned partners, unaligned places. We may even resist engaging in experiences that make us feel better, knowing that scrolling social media will lift our mood only momentarily, whereas moving our body or having a good cry can help us regulate on a deeper level. The same goes for fear. Understanding what healthy fear or discomfort feels like versus what a resounding "no" feels like is a powerful insight. It can impact the things we consume, certain experiences we have, what we choose to prioritize, and who we are as individuals.

Our emotions are messengers, and if we choose not to listen to them, we abdicate a powerful gift of being human—our awareness. We stop choosing ourselves. We lose track of who we are in this big, vast, and noisy world. We disconnect from our inner landscapes and inevitably struggle with making decisions that best support our unique and beautifully individualized selves. We reject our existence. We cage our spirit. We give up our freedom.

If we look at the world of positive psychology—which focuses on flourishing emotionally, mentally, and physically—we see the value in feeling the full range of our emotions. Emotional intelligence is defined by the Oxford dictionary as "the capacity to be aware of, control and express one's emotions, and to handle interpersonal relationships judiciously and empathetically." As Emiliya Zhivotovskaya, founder of the Flourishing Center, explains, "Emotional intelligence is marked by noticing, naming and navigating emotions within yourself and others." This builds resilience and leads to better understanding of the self and others.

Why we choose to value feeling—even, or especially, when it's anything but easy—is a question that can impact everything we touch. It starts a conversation within. This affects what we bring into our relationships, how we respond to conflict, the way we interact with strangers, how we navigate adversity and tragedy, the work we choose, the way we show up, the impact we have, and most of all, the relationship we have with ourselves.

It's important to note that along with giving ourselves permission to be human, it's imperative that we also give ourselves grace and the permission to fail. This is hard work, and along with this work come missteps, mistakes, and mishaps. It requires courage to begin and compassion for ourselves as we move through this very nonlinear world. But, oh, the saturation and expansion that fills our lives when we allow ourselves to feel it all. When it comes to "the work," Clarissa Pinkola Estés says it best in her book *Women Who Run with the Wolves*: "The challenge of loving unappealing aspects of ourselves is as much of an endeavor as any heroine [or hero] has ever undertaken."

I see it as one of the worthiest endeavors, and I have a feeling you do, too. Or at the very least, you're intrigued by the prospect of what navigating this process could look like for you.

So let's start there. ✑

full-bodied

Rich • Complex • Multifaceted

Full-bodied emotions are how they sound—they take up space in our full bodies. They can feel all-encompassing, big, loud, and intense. Like all emotions, these feelings are neither good nor bad. Fear may meet us before doing something daring. Anxiety reminds us we care about something. Love takes up space in every crevice and every cell. They show up differently for everyone, but regardless of how they make themselves known, we feel them throughout our entire being. Much like full-bodied wine or food, they're rich and complex, and their beauty lies in our ability to connect with this. What wisdom is here for you? How do these emotions add saturation and depth to your life?

Loneliness

Loneliness walks by my side when I wish she wouldn't.

When I want some quiet.

When the wind blows through the trees and my shoulders hang a little lower.

Loneliness walks by my side when I want to be alone. That's the funny part, really. Being alone would be so much better than being lonely.

Her presence is agitating, a reminder that something is missing.

Or someone.

And although there is no malice, there is pain. A sweet poisonous feeling. The feeling of alcohol settling into your limbs—warm but rendering her prey unable to move fluidly and coherently. I wonder if it's a coincidence that *loneliness* and *lioness* are three letters off.

Regardless of my feelings for her, Loneliness is here, and we walk together. She's loyal, I'll give her that. She stays close, her lavender hair long and straight. Her footsteps light and gentle. Her pale skin glowing against the silver-colored sweater she wears like a cloak.

She's graceful and mysterious; beautiful in a haunting way.

Like the moon on fog-filled nights.

A common word said over and over until it sounds foreign and abstract.

Or your own image in the mirror when you look up quickly and so clearly see yourself; candid and bare-boned.

Eventually, the two of us walk the city streets long enough that they lead us to Loneliness's painted door, where yet another silvery hue meets us. We turn the doorknob and enter.

Loneliness's favorite color is silver. It was the first thing I noticed—a theme throughout her modern apartment, passing neutral tones and pastel elements. It has a cooling element to it—almost too cool. My body aches for warmth.

The truth is, I spend little time at Loneliness's abode, a fact I feel lucky and privileged to own. But even when I do find myself sitting in her dark-raspberry-colored wool armchair, we rarely speak. What is there to say? In a roomful of people, Loneliness stands tall and still. She reverberates off the walls. Open your mouth to speak, and the facade is broken; no amount of people can dim her metallic might.

What marvels me is what a force of nature she is. For someone of so few words, of such small movements, she leaves a big wake in her midst. She summons silence and somehow makes it unbearably loud—each honk on the city street mocks me.

But when I do sit still and stay close, when I take her hand on those long walks through the night, her cold touch keeps me awake and aware. Loneliness herself keeps good company until I gain clarity on what it is I need.

Or who I need.

Sometimes, the person I need ends up being me. A connection with myself is crucial if I want to connect to others. I think that's why once I leave Loneliness's side, I feel fuller. Because in a roomful of people, I need myself first. And Loneliness to remind me of that.

This is what I realize as I sit in her dimly lit apartment and look outside at the night air.

I've never noticed the moon shine as brightly as it does on the nights when I visit Loneliness.

Sorrow

Sorrow's house is midnight blue with white shutters decorated with crescent-moon cutouts.

She lives amid the fog most days in an ethereal haze, giving the impression that her home is floating. On easier days, I find this to be poetic. But on days when I can barely lift my eyes to the world around me, feeling untethered in Sorrow's space has me grasping frantically for something to hold on to.

Sorrow's home sits up on a cliff overlooking the ocean. A proud and regal lighthouse stands firm and steady in the distance. Its light is mellow and soft. It circles around, disappearing for a moment and reappearing the next. Most times, I never doubt the light will return. My breath continues on, deep and trusting, until that beam of light hits me right between the eyes. But there are darker moments when I arrive at Sorrow's door—nights when I've been delaying my arrival. Laced with a pain that brings me to my knees, I barely notice the light at all.

When I visit Sorrow, she knows to say very little. Sorrow is incredible at holding space, for she understands that the only way is through. She can feel the deep pools of energy I access to cross the threshold of her home. And she knows that although I need space, I don't want to be alone.

My entrance into Sorrow's home varies. Sometimes, I stumble in, accidently knocking over mugs handmade out of speckled brown clay, spilling warm, spicy tea on the floor, creating a cacophony in my wake. Other times, I walk in with grace and with pride, knowing that Sorrow's home is exactly where I need to be to feel at peace again.

This particular evening, I come in aware and awake. Circumstances have led me here—a recent loss has warranted a trip to see her. I've gotten to know Sorrow in a more intimate sense these past couple of years. I've noticed the way her gorgeous gray hair shimmers in the dewy light emanating from a candle nearing the end of its life. I've found a whole world in her smile, a softness in her embrace, and a heartbreak in her voice as it coos like a mourning dove. Sorrow has been magnificent, multifaceted like a crystal, and full of so much love. It's the love, I've noticed, that's made visiting her so painstakingly hard and intrinsically desired at the same time.

Sorrow has left me fresh-baked oatmeal cookies and warm cinnamon milk. A breeze blows her hand-laced curtains quietly through the open window overlooking the sea.

These elements are intentionally placed more as a welcoming gesture than anything else, for all I want to do when I enter Sorrow's space is climb the stairs, throw myself on the bed, close my eyes, and sleep.

Sometimes, I spend what feels like days here in a groggy rest. I navigate gut-wrenching waves of grief, crying out in my sleep. I feverishly study fragments of meaning from my dreams, catching tiny gems while the rest of the sand falls through the cracks of my fingers. I am integrating Sorrow gently, lovingly, realistically into my bones—making space for her to rest alongside me.

It's here that my fever finally breaks, with Sorrow at my side. Her cold skin holds mine. Her steady breathing quiets the noise. And I can feel that I'm held. Here, in this entanglement of emotion, Sorrow holds me and whispers ever so gently in my ear, "It's okay, you're okay. It'll be day soon."

As the morning light peeks through the window, I breathe a little steadier. Sorrow is downstairs now; I hear her moving with purpose throughout the kitchen. I smell cinnamon again. And I notice my hunger has returned.

Life is full of Sorrow, I realize. But that's because it's full of love, of meaning, of beauty. Sorrow is simply the guardian of a heart that is fully alive.

I stretch my legs and my arms before sitting up and looking outside across the sparkling ocean.

A glint from the lighthouse refracting off the water meets my eyes, and I inhale, drawing it deeply into my lungs.

Grief

Your name arrived in my mind this morning, clear, as though someone had spoken it out loud, and I knew Grief was on her way. That long white hair would haunt me for some time to come.

The first time I met Grief, I noticed my watch stopped working. No number of taps on its glass surface would start it again. Grief stole time, and when I realized that, I felt sick.

It was beyond a sickness, really. It didn't heal the same way a head cold does. It didn't break like a fever. It was a part of me now—I knew that, whether I liked it or not. Grief knew this, too, but it didn't seem to bother her much.

When I first lost you, Grief and I never really spoke. Much like Loneliness and I did, we walked side by side without ever making intimate eye contact. We coexisted in stolen side glances. She was a wisp—elusive and sharp. She flattened life with a "before and after" and the jarring realization that things would never be the way they once were. Colors dripped away, my senses dulled. And although I'd participate in the life before me, it mocked me with every new day we wouldn't have together.

As time passed, and healing took its rightful place, Grief and I began to speak. We talked of love, of life, and of pain. She'd braid a few strands of her hair as she spoke, a nervous albeit endearing tick of hers, and I'd listen, with a heart that opened slowly and surely.

Soon, it was your voice that began to flood my body. I'd hear it again and it would bring me to my knees. But it was there—clear and vibrating off the walls. And in that moment, I found gratitude that time had stopped, just to hear you once more. It lived on when you didn't.

In these moments, Grief would hold more space for me than anyone I have met. She would hold the anger, the ferocious pain, the animalistic aches, and the deep joy I carried for our life together. She understood how nonlinear this path is and never expected me to show up at a certain time on a certain day. She never expected anything of me, really. Just to feel. And feel. And feel.

And when feeling became too much, she held my thrashing body and soothed my burning throat and, much like Sorrow, reminded me that this was love persevering. And in that sense, you would never truly be gone.

Grief shows me a version of myself as raw and stripped as the day I entered this world. She reminds me of who I am and the beauty of a dual existence. She reminds me of you.

So, when I hear your name again, I pause what I'm doing to watch the clock and count down the seconds until it stops.

I know the white hair isn't far behind.

And I can't wait to hear your voice.

Rage

Rage writes his name in all capitals. He likes tequila on the rocks. Rage leaves my throat feeling coarse. And my hands shaking.

My dad introduced him to me as a child, and together they made big, loud, alarming shadow puppets against a white wall on a hot night in the middle of summer.

In my life, Rage has been a source of pain and shame. He's also been a source of liberation and power, which is what makes my relationship with him inherently complex. He kept the little girl—who grew so cold that her teeth chattered and her skin sank—warm and breathing. He lit the fire inside of a child when that fire was barely flickering. He reminded her that she, too, mattered.

This, among other reasons I'm still figuring out, is why I frequent his place more than I'd like to admit.

I can see the desert skyline from his window. Purple mountains majesty stare back at me, making me wish that I could see a color other than red. But in true fashion, Rage's Airstream is a dusty, worn-out red with hints of aged copper subtly shining through. His space is a bit manic and a bit disheveled; piles of magazines against the wall and a half-filled dustpan propped up next to a broom reveal themselves proudly. I wonder why he doesn't throw away the clutter. I wonder if in some strange way it fills the space and superficially makes him feel less lonely.

My favorite moments of meeting Rage are when I catch him off guard. I find him hunkered over a workbench in a shed out back, forging steel, deep in alchemic creation. The smell of burning metal invites me in. The sparks of orange and crimson make me stay. Watching Rage so focused as he channels his pains, his past lives, and his inner fire into melting metal—twisting and turning it into new shapes—makes me feel alive.

As we build intimacy and trust, Rage allows me to peel back his layers one by one. We speak of Grief, the girl he grew up next door to and often longs for. We speak of Fairness, his best friend, who means well but is sometimes flaky, something that really sets Rage off. And we speak of Loneliness, a wisp, if you will, that keeps Rage up at night and may be the only person that can make him feel ice cold.

We also speak about us, which feels good and long overdue. I confess that, to this day, he floods my body with adrenaline, and I still fight with loud wails and fat tears and beads of sweat.

But amid our conversation, Rage softens. He leans his solid body close to mine. He smiles.

"You aren't that little girl anymore," he says calmly. "I may have helped save you then, but now you save yourself. You'll burn up if you live with me for too long, darling. You can take the heat, no doubt. But life blooms in the open air. Feel me, and then breathe me out. After all, when in balance, the air is what keeps the fire steady."

I have forever grappled with this notion that there's a time and place for Rage, but screaming at the top of my lungs and burning everything around me only keeps me blinded by smoke and choking for air—the same air that can set me free.

That little girl now lives on inside me, at home, tending to the fire. She knows how it feels in her body when boundaries are violated or when she's mistreated; Rage showed her. What a gift that is. What precious responsibility to hold. With that wisdom, the fire burns on. But it's no longer lit as a means of survival. Rage is important and will forever be a part of me. But never again will I need to indulge in a bottomless tequila to prove myself. After all, there is no worm at the bottom of that bottle.

The sun drops and the nighttime desert air sneaks through the slightly cracked windows in his home. Rage stretches, rubs his bristled face in his hands, and nods. That's my cue to get going.

I throw back the last sip of tequila in my glass, licking my lips, which taste of salt and lime, and gently close the door behind me.

The air hits my face, and as I turn to leave, I can hear metal transforming, much like my narrative.

And I take a breath.

It's the coolness lining my lungs that guides me home tonight.

Failure

take a deep breath as I look out at the beach and listen to the waves fall quietly on the shore, as though to whisper secrets to the sand and then quickly take them back.

I always meet Failure on the beach. It's his favorite place to come.

He told me it was because he likes to watch the lines in the sand disappear as the waves take them back out to sea, erasing what we think we know and replacing it with something new.

As I let out a breath, I turn to my right and see him walking up the beach. His head bobs back and forth, and his rusty-red bucket hat, faded from the sun, sits lightly on his shaggy hair, which covers part of his eyes. He is tall and lanky in a seriously sweet way, almost giving the appearance that he is clumsy. But Failure is anything but clumsy. He is smart, precise, and always on time.

When he reaches me, a huge smile spreads across his face, and he takes a seat on the sand next to me. I have become less anxious about meeting Failure, something that has evolved as I've grown and aged and become more intimate with him. I have so many great memories of us in my childhood, learning how to ride a bike or tie my shoes. When I hit my teenage and college years, Failure felt more ominous; as if tied to my identity, bound to the sides of my young heart. As an adult, I experience moments when Failure brings me to my knees, with my hands covered in wet sand and the spray from the rocky sea leaving me shivering and empty.

But with time, I come to see him for who he is. He's reliable, no matter how long I try to stay away.

"Hey there, sweet pea," he says, removing his hat and dusting off the sand between his hands. "Beautiful day today, eh?"

I nod and smile back as I tousle his hair.

He reaches slowly into his pocket and pulls something out. In his hands he holds a box made of shells; shiny and iridescent, they feel sacred and true, like holding a piece of the moon.

"For me?" I ask.

"As always," he replies.

Failure's findings are wrapped up in an intricate paper of bright orange and deep emerald. I know that meeting him is a token to be held with regard. Amid lost direction and grief, Failure reminds me that I've tried, that I've grown, and that I've learned something in the process.

He is a way of life, a reminder that I chose the vulnerable choice and how beautifully brave that is. Failure's gifts are priceless, and although the shells are jagged and prickly, they'll smooth out over time.

I thank him for his gift, hug him tight, and start to head home. As I walk away, I play with the necklace around my neck that displays every shell I've ever received from him. I softly touch them and turn back to wave goodbye one last time, but all I see are those waves again—writing melodies in the sand and taking them away with each stroke.

And a rusty-red bucket hat placed quietly on the shore.

Longing

Sitting with Longing always leaves me feeling internally damp.

The vast jungle that grows inside—creating live walls on the sides of my rib cage—is too much to bear sometimes.

I find myself tucked into a ball against a windowsill listening to a combination of soft piano and white noise, deeply involved in Longing's profound and somewhat ethereal company.

There is something beautiful about Longing. I watch him spin the tops of wineglasses ever so slightly so that a humming sound enters the room as I settle deeper into the feeling of living two lives at once. A limbo for the soul.

"Gratitude," he says, breaking the lilac haze that hangs in the air. The smell of falling rain dances in my chest, feeding my internal rain forest.

I open my eyes, realizing for the first time that I've melted into his dreamlike presence.

"It's what brings me back when I get too caught up in myself."

I nod, understanding exactly what he means. That moment when you choose your life. The moment when you have everything you need. And want.

Longing goes back to his wineglasses, and I close my eyes, resting my head against the foggy window; a picture book of my life passing before me.

And my smile grows bigger by the second.

Temptation

Temptation is a woman.

I know this because I can see her silhouette through the window as I pass by her house.

Darkened shapes move slowly against smoky coral light.

Her curves are siren songs.

To enter her home is to be lost in ecstasy. An unrolling of the tongue. A quickening of the breath. An opening of the legs.

And mind.

Temptation leads me into the rooms of her home—reflection, restoration, and relief. Thrilling me, intriguing me.

And yet as a young woman, I would often leave her home with rosy cheeks and messy hair—itchy with shame. Everything I'd been taught about Temptation, as well as her sister, Sensuality, told me that pleasure and feeling oneself were wrong and unacceptable.

On one night in particular, I walked into Temptation's home and let her lead me into her studio, complete with an easel in the corner, where a freshly stretched canvas wore a fresh coat of splatted paint, and smoke from a recently blown-out candle lingered. The lighting was warm. The air was cool. My eyes were open.

To sit and stay with her is to unravel in the most seductive way. A coming home long overdue.

What they forget to tell you is that it was Temptation who filled women with curiosity, audacity, and self-assurance. It was Temptation who plucked the apple from the tree, handed it to Eve, and said, "Here—be free." Temptation is empowerment incarnate.

On foggy nights, Temptation slips out into the streets.

I know this because I meet her there.

She hands me a mirror each time, reminding me to feed myself with the intimacy I so crave. She takes my hand and places it on my skin. There is a warmth to the touch that signifies a wild undercurrent of life—an entire internal landscape waiting to be acknowledged.

"There," she says, looking me in the eyes, "is where we begin."

Anxiety

Outside Anxiety's house hangs a copper number 5 and 2, perfectly aligned. You wouldn't know externally that the energy shifts once your foot steps over the threshold. I got to know Anxiety well during postpartum. We talked so frequently, and when we did, it was so frantic that I couldn't catch my breath. I found myself gasping when we were together. The air is different in that house.

He likes his food spicy. Carolina Reapers grow in his backyard. I one time made the mistake of peeling them bare-handed and spent the next six hours moaning and writhing in pain as the oils nestled into my fingertips. I fell asleep with milk-drenched hands.

As I get to know Anxiety in an intimate way, I see his intentions are not unkind. He means well. I don't blame him for my not being able to sometimes decipher where he ends and where I begin—I knew from a young age that it's my job to figure that out. I have no interest in trying to cast out Anxiety; I know that's an unfair expectation. But I had long ago decided that Anxiety and I would not have a codependent relationship.

One night, I sat on his couch hazy-eyed, noticing the fluorescent sign that read OPEN 24/7; it hung in his living room in typical bachelor-pad style and made me cringe. Its warm red light softly coated the off-white paint on the wall behind it. On. Off. On, off. A pulsing though silent alarm. The more I watched it, the more I could feel Anxiety's presence. It may have been silent in the beginning, but now it was blaring. I scrambled around the room, my hands clasped tightly over my ears, searching for the off button, but I couldn't find it. It was in that moment that Anxiety found me crouched on the floor, took my body in his, and let out a deep breath. The alarm stopped. The light dimmed. And I could hear again.

That's the thing about Anxiety—his presence alone is to be human. To feel fear, to worry, to live a life of awareness. He's here when something important is on the line; he reminds me I care. He wants me to be safe, to feel secure. He reveals my needs and has no interest in keeping me captive or shoving hot peppers down my throat.

He wants me to know this.

And I do.

I have the pepper seeds in my pocket to prove it.

Passion

Crystal-blue eyes.

That thick bottom lip.

An overflowing heart and seemingly boundless self.

Controlling my body when I'm around Passion feels like I'm trying to keep still while treading water.

The truth is, I don't want to control myself around him. I daydream about moments we'll spend together—sweaty, entangled, and speechless. He lives deep inside my belly, moving up and down my legs as he gets closer.

It's how I know he's on his way.

My relationship with Passion becomes more refined as I grow older. Interests, desires, and people enter my life, and there he is with that deep voice and a hand on the small of my back.

Witnessing him come alive through other people—their stories, mannerisms, and ways of being—is intoxicating. I watch the desert sun set and rise right beside him; the room is sticky, his skin is hot, and my heart is all in.

Having an outlet with Passion is how we cocreate; an outlet to express, to be free, to be wild. Without any space for us to live fiercely, he sticks to the sides of my lungs, and I spend the day chasing my breath. I lose my footing and the desert feels vast and vague, filling to the brim with nowhere to land, about to implode.

But with presence and a grounded focus, Passion brings life alive. He teaches me to want courageously, to care deeply, and to understand why certain places and people make me want to shed my skin and reveal a deeper layer of self.

He illuminates the parts of life that drive me mad in the best possible way—pen to paper, how the body speaks and loves in a million different ways. He plays me piano and sings me to sleep.

So, when I find myself in his dimly lit desert home nestled underneath the bright night sky, I exhale, close my eyes, and surrender to his coarse hair between my fingers.

And a deep warmth that never cools.

Fear

was wrapped up in a tartan wool blanket in Fear's house. The fire behind me warmed my back, allowing each muscle along my spine to relax.

There was a strange comfort here. When you've visited Fear as many times as I have, it becomes a routine, and that routine becomes a guarantee. In a world full of unknowns, sometimes it's easier to bask by the fire at Fear's place than to venture out into the winter air.

It was the kind of comfort where you forget that you don't belong. A bodily alert comes every few seconds; even though your mind thinks this is the place to rest your bones forever, your body nudges you to run.

Leg jerks.

A twitch of the wrist.

Like when you're falling asleep and you jump out of your skin, your body trying desperately to keep you alive.

I knew this feeling of my body and mind being at war. And so, I sat with it as Fear stammered on in the background about his opinions and what-ifs in the world.

Fear always has a lot to say.

His face was worn and wrinkled, with wire eyeglass frames that sat on the bridge of his nose; his head was full of thick white hair. He was tall and skinny, gaunt, and smelled of eucalyptus oil. There was little about Fear that was disarming. He quickened my heart and rearranged my vocal cords so that panic rang clear in my voice; a barren branch in the dead of winter scraping against a pane of glass.

Many times, I've felt wildly unsafe in his company—like all that mattered to me in the world would soon be lost.

But like us all, Fear needs a place to talk, a space to be himself. And as hard as it is at times, I lend a listening ear.

I just always make sure to leave his energy in his house before closing the door and heading home to mine. He's a part of me, I know. In a world full of forests and deserts, beaches and cities, homes and new spaces to be, Fear lives, but so do so many other emotions. And so do I.

Fear's home is disorderly yet still has a sense of reason to it. Empty suitcases sit contently against a wall, stacked on top of one another. And next to them is a table of fully used passports, stamps covering the sheets inside. Résumés litter his floor, and I flip through half-written books that create a sort of side table, complete with a small ceramic vase that sits on top, filled with a few sprigs of thyme.

"Ah," I said out loud as Fear stopped midsentence and turned to look at me. "The trips no one took and the adventures so many chose."

Fear smiled at me. He's always appreciated my talent for reading a room, and of course my insight into him.

"It's true what they say about me," he said as he removed his glasses, pulled out a cloth, and circled it around and around the lenses. "I'm a challenge to move through, but when done, I can be expansive. I'm often loud and not always rooted in logic, but I can show you what you want, what you need, and what's important to you. I can keep you safe. To be alive is to know me."

He put his glasses back on and returned to stammering about his ancestors, siblings, and grandkids that lived so prominently throughout our world, but I could no longer hear him.

My mind was filled with the sound of my mother's voice humming in the early morning as I lay in my childhood bed safe and sound.

Before Fear had ever wrapped his tartan blanket around my shoulders. And spread fire into my veins.

Workbook Pages for
full-bodied

STEP 1: GREET

You feel an emotion is present. Say hello and acknowledge that it's here while doing your best not to attach judgment or try to change it, fix it, or remove it. Let it take up space. You can do this. Your body can hold it all.

Now, you can name it. Hello, ... *. Welcome.*

In my body

You feel like . . .

. . . .

. . . .

. . . .

. . . .

. . . .

You taste like . . .

....

.

....

....

....

....

....

You smell like . . .

....

....

....

....

....

....

You make me want to . . .

....

....

....

....

....

....

....

As a messenger

You teach me . . .

. . . .

. . . .

. . . .

. . . .

. . . .

. . . .

You show me . . .

. . . .

. . . .

. . . .

. . . .

. . . .

. . . .

You need this to feel seen and heard . . .

. . . .

. . . .

. . . .

. . . .

. . . .

. . . .

Your secret is . . .

. . . .

. . . .

. . . .

. . . .

. . . .

. . . .

. . . .

IF YOU NEED A RAINCHECK:

You need me to make space for you right now, but I don't have the time, accessibility, or availability at the moment. I have a sweet little sun-filled room where you can sit and wait. I'll be back. In the meantime, know that I see you and I'm here to listen.

Time I'll be back:

. . . .

. . . .

. . . .

. . . .

. . . .

. . . .

. . . .

STEP 2: SIT

Hi, it's me. I'm here and ready to sit down to get to know you better. I know you have messages to share and ways to help me grow and heal. Let's sit together and discover the reason for your visit.

What activating event (an experience or a trigger) has currently introduced me to this emotion?

....

....

....

....

....

....

Right after the activating event and before I found myself with this emotion, there's a voice. This can be a belief or a story—something we tell ourselves either out of conditioning or previous experiences. What does this voice or this story say?

....

....

....

....

....

....

How does this story make me feel?

. . . .

. . . .

. . . .

. . . .

. . . .

. . . .

. . . .

. . . .

. . . .

And how does this emotion cause me to react?

. . . .

. . . .

. . . .

. . . .

. . . .

. . . .

. . . .

. . . .

. . . .

How can I honor exactly how I feel? How can I respect what I need most in this moment?

....
....
....
....
....
....
....
....

What is one thing I can do for myself while I'm feeling this emotion that will bring me nourishment? What feels safe here?

....
....
....
....
....
....
....
....
....
....

STEP 3: CONVERSE

I'm glad we decided to sit down. It may not have been easy or simple, but it created space to understand each other better. It's time for a heart-to-heart.

Time to cue into my senses: Is it cold or warm? Does a breeze blow, or is it humid and thick? What do I feel on my skin when I close my eyes? What do I taste in the air? What smells draw me in? What colors stand out to me?

Where is our meeting place? Am I at my emotion's home, or do we meet somewhere else? Describe the landscape.

....
....
....
....
....
....
....
....
....

What does their home look like? Is their front door ornate or plain? Explain the exterior of their home and what surrounds it.

....
....
....
....
....
....
....
....
....
....

When I step inside their house, what textures do I find? What aesthetic themes emerge? Does it feel warm and cozy or minimalistic and drab? Is there food cooking or the scent of flowers on the table? What stands out to me about stepping into their world?

....

....

....

....

....

....

....

....

When I see the emotion, what does he/she/they look like? What feels striking about them?

....

....

....

....

....

....

....

....

....

What is their disposition? Are they kind? Jovial? Rugged? Quiet?

....

....

....

....

....

....

....

....

....

....

Do they have a hobby? What do they love to do? What makes them come alive?

....

....

....

....

....

....

....

....

....

....

What hurts them, scares them, worries them?

What about them surprises me? Speak to their duality.

What stories do they share? What past lives do I learn about? What do they need me to know? Write some dialogue.

What is one element about our time together that feels important or stands out?

Is there a shifted perspective and/or physical item(s) I walk away with that reminds me of our time together?

. . . .

. . . .

. . . .

. . . .

. . . .

. . . .

. . . .

. . . .

. . . .

What is this emotion here to tell me?

. . . .

. . . .

. . . .

. . . .

. . . .

. . . .

. . . .

. . . .

. . . .

What is one thing I can do right now to help myself and this emotion feel more loved, seen, and accepted?

STEP 4: GRATITUDE AND GOODBYE

I am so grateful for you because you are a part of me. And I am so grateful for me because I am here—growing, committing, and recommitting, messy and disheveled and present. I am a human, and for that I applaud myself. This is my thank-you letter to my emotion and to myself. I acknowledge us for who we are as fully as I can—always holding the easy, the hard, and everything in between.

What insight(s) did I uncover that I'd like to thank my emotion for leading me to?

....

....

....

....

....

....

....

....

....

....

....

....

What part of my emotion and myself am I able to shed a softer light on?

What newfound gratitude do I have for myself and my emotion?

What story was I able to reframe about this emotion?

How does this new thought/perspective make me feel?

When I alchemize/process this emotion, what other supportive emotions do I have access to?

How has **this** process shifted the way I react/respond to feeling this emotion, whether toward myself or toward someone else?

Creating boundaries within our relationships is what keeps them centered in respect and nurtured with care, both for ourselves and the person we're in a relationship with. Our emotions are no different. While we want to acknowledge, embrace, and express our feelings, it's essential that we also know when it's time to pause until we meet again.

When we feel stuck, whether in the form of avoidance or in the form of rumination, we halt the natural ebb and flow of emotions. When we do this, we're attaching to the story we've created about ourselves and our emotion versus witnessing the emotion, processing it, and allowing it to move through. The truth is, we are story-driven creatures hardwired to weave stories to understand our experience—we are *Homo narrativus*. The challenge isn't in having a story, but the picture that story paints and how we can (depending on our experiences and our healing) react or respond to that picture. It begins with bringing ourselves back into our bodies, into the present moment. It begins with coming home to ourselves.

As humans, we're in the business of feeling. Reframing—choosing a new perspective or belief about ourselves and our emotion that's supportive of our well-being—gives us a chance to step back and look at our own triggers without casting blame on ourselves. It helps give clarity as to why our triggers and emotions are present and what they say about our life experiences and our needs. It can help restore empathy, confidence, and self-trust. It can boost humanity. And most of all, it helps us validate our own emotional experiences. By choosing to validate ourselves, we claim ourselves.

This is not to be confused with emotional bypassing or, in cases of abuse or systemic discrimination, where external circumstances play a very real role. And it's not to say that we can intellectualize our way out of feeling an emotion. With any practice, awareness is key. As Brackett explains in *Permission to Feel*, "When it comes to reappraisal, we need to ask ourselves: Am I doing this simply to justify avoiding a difficult, sensitive problem? Am I doing this because I know that addressing the issue is going to lead to a long, tortured, anguished conversation?" Consistent check-ins, honesty, and respect for all that we feel is how we continue to show up in this work.

Our acknowledgment for our emotions doesn't always need to be done with love or celebration. It can be. It's wonderful when it is. But neutrality works as well. Over-identifying with any emotion disrupts the natural evolution of our feelings and ultimately leads us away from ourselves; this is the case for both difficult and pleasant emotions alike.

Psychologists Lahnna I. Catalino, Sara B. Algoe, and Barbara L. Fredrickson agree: Happiness is a delicate art. Studies show that prioritizing positivity leads to positive emotions and is a worthwhile pursuit. However, consistently analyzing whether you're happy or not can have the opposite effect and deprive us of a more pervasive sense of well-being. Believing that happiness is the only emotion worth experiencing, or as many refer to as toxic positivity, adds judgment to every other emotion we feel on the way to feeling joyful. It values the outcome over the journey, can cause a fixed mindset instead of a growth mindset, limits flexibility, decreases awareness, may cause us to ignore deep-rooted trauma, can perpetuate automatic negative thoughts (ANT),

and ultimately, it denies a human experience that connects us to ourselves and to others.

Feeling stuck in or avoiding harder emotions can also cause disease and a feeling of disconnection. Studies show that dwelling in negative emotions and the stress they create "produces inflammation through cytokines" and can weaken our immune systems, elevate our blood pressure, increase levels of stress hormones, and perpetuate suicidal ideation. Emotions and our relationship to them affect our entire body from the central nervous system to the immune system, endocrine system, and cardiovascular system.

We'll never get rid of "negative" emotions, nor should we try. The goal of emotional regulation, "which involves monitoring, tempering, and modifying emotional reactions in helpful ways, in order to reach personal and professional goals," is not to numb ourselves or shame ourselves for feeling. It's also not about micromanaging or controlling our emotions. And as we've discussed, it's certainly not in our best interest to ignore or reject negative emotions and put our energy into only feeling positive ones. Emotional regulation lives in the space where we give ourselves and others the permission to own and feel our feelings—the entire spectrum.

In my own practice, a big part of self-regulation is sensing my body and remembering the stillness that lives there. Somatic teacher Varvara Erochina explains it best when she says, "Emotional regulation is an embodied skill developed through practice—both alone and through attunement with other people. It requires a combination of dropping into our bodies, developing new neural pathways, nervous system capacity, and shifting the conscious and subconscious stories we have about feelings." We tend to our inner home by pruning the roses, making a cup of tea, and sitting down by the fire. We allow ourselves to arrive for a moment before inviting a guest into the house or before putting our boots on to leave.

Studies show that self-regulation or emotional regulation also attributes to better psychological adjustment, less psychopathology, higher self-compassion and self-confidence, less addiction, more impactful relationships, improved interpersonal skills, and stronger secure attachment.

Even in knowing all of this, sometimes saying goodbye is hard. Sometimes, we find power or comfort in an emotion. Anger may remind us of our self-worth, and saying goodbye to that emotion means releasing the newly found empowerment it revealed. But if we stay in anger for too long, we begin to lash out at others, disconnecting ourselves from love, forgiveness, and intimacy. We spiral inward, shut down, and cut ourselves off.

As Clarissa Pinkola Estés explains in *Women Who Run with the Wolves*, "Dwelling on trauma and doing so intensely for a period of time is very important to healing. But eventually all injury has to be given sutures and be allowed to heal over into scar tissue." So, how do we know when to say goodbye? Emotional regulation is a tool we discover more throughout the workbook pages in this journal using our creativity and prompts alongside our intuition. Like anything, it's a muscle we can strengthen through awareness, reflection, and experience. ✐

groovy

Electric · Free-Spirited · Vibrant

Groovy emotions are colorful, free-spirited, and strong-willed. They make us want to get up and move; they inspire us to take action in ways both big and small. They're electric and vibrant in nature; they buzz beneath our skin. Always brimming with a sense of style, they meet us on city streets, leisurely bike rides, and in newly adopted hobbies. Spending time with them helps us better understand what brings us joy and what lights us up.

Moxie

oxie looks how her name sounds—spunky and peppy,
with a contagious laugh and a bad habit of chewing her
nails. She wears her blond hair in a pixie cut, which ac-
centuates her strong cheekbones and doll-like green eyes.
She has inexhaustible joie de vivre. And she knows it.

She is small in stature, but it fools no one who befriends her. She's
scrappy, strong-willed, and incredibly resourceful; often offering to cut
her friends' hair or wallpaper their home without any previous practice
or experience. Being beside her feels exciting and motivating. Being beside her makes me feel invincible.

We were ships in the night when I was younger; my motivation for
befriending her was always changing alongside my interests and hobbies.
Sometimes, it was to impress a crush; other times, it was for approval
from family. But Moxie and I are closest when I'm pursuing things for
myself as a way of being me. She's not one for power trips or ego boosts.

We reunited when I moved to San Francisco. Not at first, as most of my intimate friends took time to find, like a signature scent or the places that feel like home.

She journeyed with me to the center of the city, where I attended design school, and was with me the first time I took a bus across town, determined to immerse myself in my city and the people who inhabited it. She was there when I got our dog and moved into a new apartment and when I started a new job—all within the same week. She was also there when I quit that job two years later as a means of respecting my boundaries and my worth. She's the cousin of Courage, but Moxie has more style, more swagger. She's the voice in my head that says, "Do you want it? Then let's get to it." She's the reason I trust in my dreams. She's vitality incarnate.

Today, I meet Moxie at our favorite hole-in-the-wall—a Vietnamese restaurant just outside the Russian Hill district. No one speaks English and the food is some of the best we've ever eaten. It feels good to be here, to be emerged in another culture, even if only momentarily. Moxie agrees. She loves eating in silence without the pressure of having to hold a conversation. "I'm free to be" is what she says between bites of five-spice duck and bun cha.

That's what I love about Moxie—her nerve to show up as she is, her determination to go after what she wants, and her spirit to take her through the process. She had the grit and drive to actualize dreams. And she allowed life—or Vietnamese food—to happen along the way.

We walk for a little while up and down the San Francisco hills, admiring the quirky life that lives on around us, and buy lychee from street vendors in Chinatown until we are out of breath and sticky with fruit juice. The day goes on and on with Moxie by my side, but I know it's time I take some of her energy and focus on my own goals.

She knows this, too, for she kisses me on both cheeks, waves goodbye, and walks straight into the California sun, threatening to outshine it on her way.

Possibility

watch as Possibility twists and twists a piece of her copper-colored hair around her finger. It sends chills up my spine. But I know not to flee from Possibility; she's taught me how to free-fall beside her and trust where it takes me.

I feel something and look down to see Possibility grabbing my hand. Her skin is softer than I imagined. Her nail polish an electric blue. Her smile is big and fearless, drawing everything in with its thirst for life; a black hole for the lucky. Her red hair is long and thick and wild, the kind of hair that feels sensual. The kind of hair you want to pull.

If I look away for a second, I swear that she'll blur into the city sky-line.

The music gets louder, and I watch her thick-soled, glossy black leather boots move up and down, side to side; a kind of Morse code that only the curious can understand and appreciate.

I open my eyes and the room comes into view. The city lives on in flashes of light in the background. "Play with us," it says. "Come. Seek."

We run through the apartment building, out the heavy double doors, and into the night. The air feels cool against my cheeks. Her hands feel warm on my face.

And just like that, she's gone. I awake now to find myself in my own bed, a smile still plastered on my face. My hands grip the sheets. My toes move up and down. She dances inside a little while longer.

I've intertwined myself with Possibility like that piece of copper hair wrapped around her finger.

And I'm limitless.

Joy

don't remember the first time I met Joy. Looking back, I think she was
built into my cells; put there by my parents, my sister, the Gods themselves.

Even at a young age, I realized it was a privilege to know her inti-
mately. She was spoken about in velvetlike tones with such high regard.

Memories of her pour in, often sparked by watching home videos or
recalling family stories. Toddling around our backyard in a diaper, chasing my older sister, or catching fireflies on the back deck in the sticky heat
of July—they're simple moments, really. Riding a bike was my happy
place. Falling asleep on the couch next to my parents was my castle.

I knew she was there, even as a child. I could feel the air push back my
dark brown curls as I stared at a familiar face across from me on the
seesaw.

Up.

Down.

Up.

The high-pitched squeals echoed off the worn brick walls of our school.

And that's when I saw her.

She was in a crystallized form—how life looks through a kaleidoscope.

Multifaceted.

Undeniable.

Dreamy.

Joy, staring back at me, feeding me life. She had strawberry blond hair and a full smile. Her eyes, one brown and one blue, were quirky and alluring. Her voice sounded like hearing your name spoken out loud by someone who loves you. Being in her presence felt like floating weightless in a vast ocean while steady waves rocked back and forth.

On days when I raised a skeptical eye at Joy out of fear of losing the goodness she provided, she was warm and kind. She was patient. As I surrendered, I felt safe by her side, and it made every difference in the world.

So, we soared together, high into the tangerine sky. Weightless and free. And before I left the playground to skip home, she promised me she'd always be with me as long as I remembered to look.

Life went on, and sometimes, I felt as though Joy had abandoned me. Or rather, that I forgot how to choose her. At times, our relationship felt like endless moments of hide-and-seek.

But as I grew, I learned firsthand that I don't need to feel joyful in all moments to know she exists within me. When I'm in deep pain, she roams through the space in between breaths, reminding me that my heart still beats even when it's broken. During challenges or loss, she's there in the form of friends and family who scoop me up and love me over and over and over.

And in everyday moments, when a stranger on the street smiles up at me, or my child grabs my hand to lead me to the pantry for one more snack, she is a light so bright, I have to close my eyes to take her in. In these moments, she is so clear, I think I'll burst into tears from her brilliance.

After a lifetime together, I see Joy for who she is—a worthy endeavor, a friend, my heart.

And when I need her close, I allow myself to savor the air as it pushes back my curls.

The lightness of my smile.

The softness of her hand.

And know we are one.

Freedom

t is a warm April day, early in the afternoon, as I arrive inside Death Valley National Park.

I've heard of the "superbloom"—a bloom of flowers in the desert that happens once every five to ten years when conditions are just right—and I'm so eager to witness it. The plan started when Freedom called me one night with the news. "It's happening," she exclaimed, "and we're going."

I walk the trailheads, stopping to notice the teddy-bear cholla cacti, desert marigolds, and trees that look like they're straight out of a Dr. Seuss book. Soon, the smell of oranges fills my body, and I know that Freedom is close by. Her smell always gives her away.

Freedom's lofted home sits amid an orange grove, and the smell seeps into her skin. Sometimes, I laugh at the thought that she is a scratch-and-sniff in human form—orange hair that smells of oranges.

I love every second I spend with Freedom. She revives me, nourishes me, and grounds me, all at the same time. She makes me feel excited to be alive but oh so ever aware of my two feet and how grateful I am to have them on solid ground.

She brings the earth to life around her. Here we are, standing in the middle of the desert, surrounded by thousands of wildflowers reaching toward the sun. And toward Freedom.

Anything is possible when we are together.

I often think about how lucky I am to be in Freedom's company, knowing that not everyone is so privileged. It makes me sad, for Freedom feels like a birthright. When I was a child, she met me on grassy knolls during moonlit nights when fireflies hung in the air. She needs space to survive among celestial bodies and rested bones.

Our gatherings always end with a bike ride, and to honor and respect the flowers, we leave the desert and ride around her neighborhood, stopping to pick up fallen oranges. They fill my mouth with fresh, cool juice, and I laugh as we tuck them into our pockets and ride on.

When I can, I sleep over at Freedom's house and rock back and forth in the white linen hammock on her porch. It's on the second floor, surrounded by trees and the sound of the soft and subtle wind.

And as I reach my hand toward the night sky, I feel like I can scoop up the stars and bring them toward my mouth.

My hands forever smell of oranges.

Empowerment

Empowerment and I are often mistaken for sisters. We share the same almond-shaped eyes, brown in color and rich in story. We carry everything on our faces—mystery, insight, and depth. It's why we shy away from eye contact when we're feeling vulnerable. Or when we're feeling something we aren't ready to share yet.

But today I meet Empowerment on the sandy dunes by her house, and she immediately looks me in the eyes. Today, Empowerment and I are securely in our skin, wherever it takes us.

Empowerment, with her nearly black, wavy hair and olive skin, surrounds herself with her friend family, which consists of Courage, Acceptance, and Confidence. The four of them are striking in nature, all of them with an energy that makes you want to be around them.

I used to worry at first that I'd feel intimated or a sense of not belonging, but I never do. They invite me in and love me as one of their own. It's a superpower they all have, really, and I make a note to do the same for others.

Sometimes, I like to sit on the top of the dune and watch the four of them together. I focus on Empowerment and the way she stands so firmly in her power. I watch her laugh, uninhibited—her belly rolling with her full self. I watch her hug fiercely and dance freely. I watch her navigate conflict with kindness and strength, and I fall in love with her a little more with each second my eyes stay on hers.

She's met me in all situations: when advocating for myself and my child, within relationships where needs and boundaries weren't met, and when taking on exciting but nerve-racking career opportunities. But she's also there to hold my hand in the little moments: a fight with a friend, saying no, moving my body, saying "I love you," or simply accepting myself. They're all there. Empowerment and her little cohort travel far and deep for the ones they love.

The sun is high in the sky as I stretch my arms above my head. Heat waves kiss my fingertips, and I giggle, noticing the gilded nature they now carry; whispers from the sky herself. It lights up my tattoos and my heart.

Before I make my way back down the dune, I look at Empowerment below. Her almond eyes, her glistening skin, her fierceness, and her courage to show up.

And I can see it; we do look like sisters after all.

Pride

P roud like a lion," he says. He laughs a dry laugh and rolls his eyes slightly—not in a demeaning, negative way but in a playful, "how silly" sense.

"I'm all for embodied empowerment and luscious locks," he says with a smile. "But I'm more smiles than roar."

Indeed he is.

Pride is soft and gentle. He can be firm when he needs to be and isn't easily weathered, but underneath his scruffy beard and long, curly dark-blond hair, he is a gentle giant.

He stands at six feet and weighs about 180 pounds—a teddy bear in nature—and his hugs pull you completely in. I appreciate hugs like that. And I admire those who give them.

I find Pride to be misunderstood by many. So many I know see Pride as a means of doing, reaching. Many feel as though they deserve him only when they fit a certain mold. Some feel they are deserving of him if they reach perfection or fit someone else's idea of perfection. It makes me sad to see, because I know Pride for who he is—a friend to everyone.

Pride plays the saxophone and loves jazz music. He studies the history behind every artist he listens to, absorbing their wisdom and paying tribute to their life. He finds satisfaction in the process and in the teachers he learns from along the way. He is intentional, thoughtful, and steady.

I find myself at his old Victorian apartment in the city by means of a bus. I love how it feels, being a part of the people who make up the place I live. I love my city for all it is and isn't, and there is a shared kindred spirit with everyone I pass on the busy streets, whether we look up at one another or not.

Pride and I gather in his apartment to celebrate the small moments of life: when I apologize for hurting someone, when I stand my ground and tell the truth (especially if it's hard, scary, or uncomfortable), when I ask for what I need, and when I accept that I'm enough. He's there with a big smile and a pat on the back when I correct a bad habit (even in the moments I repeat it) and when I share love with someone. He's also been there for big moments: when I sent off a proposal and secured a book deal, when I experienced labor and gave birth to our son, and when I put my pain and fear aside to hold and love our sweet dog as she took her last breaths.

But above all, Pride is there to hold my hand when I misspeak, misstep, and mistake. He doesn't leave me because I err, make the wrong choice, or make a mess. He holds me with compassion and gives me space to grow in these uncomfortable but powerful areas. And when I show up at his doorstep, covered in dirt like a plant that finally broke through the soil, he shakes me off and sits me down and plays me his saxophone.

I sit here now with him. His beard is as scruffy as ever. His eyes are half opened, half closed. His mouth is pursed around his saxophone, the groovy tune fills the air, and I feel like I'm in between worlds.

But if Pride has taught me anything, it's that he is all about being, not doing. And I am just as deserving of him in the in-between as I am on solid ground.

So, I sit for a while.

And I listen.

Confidence

onfidence can be hard to pin down. I know this, for I've always been eager to find her. For years, I looked in all the wrong places—approving nods from family and friends, the shape of my body, and how good I was at "doing" certain things. Looking back, it's not surprising that I never found her there. That simply isn't where she dwells.

Once I finally met Confidence, I learned that being with her feels like being at home in one's skin while simultaneously safe enough to venture outside of it. She moves around her nineteenth-century Haussmann building—complete with a wrought-iron balcony and elaborately cut stonework—that boasts elements of a Parisian lifestyle with the art of simple enjoyment. She sits on her balcony every morning, quietly stirring her coffee as she gazes off in the distance. At what, I'm not sure, but I can tell she knows she's exactly where she belongs.

One afternoon, as I reached for an almond croissant, Confidence comfortably plopped down on the sofa across from me and sighed.

"Did you know," she said slowly and assuredly, "that sometimes I yearn for myself?"

Her vulnerability shocked and comforted me in the same breath. I sat up taller and leaned in closer, using my body language to show her that I could hold whatever she needed to share.

Confidence talked about how choosing to believe she's capable led to trusting herself and ultimately led to self-acceptance. And when Confidence reached self-acceptance, she realized she had been there all along; nothing to change, nothing to remove, nothing but a choice to be there. So, she chose herself.

And like every other human, on nights when the sun is low and a sense of rawness seems to sneak through the cracks in the wall, Confidence shutters. She rejects. She distrusts. And she casts aside. Only to wake up blanketless and bone cold in the morning.

She assured me these moments are okay because she understands that oftentimes, in order to come back home to ourselves, we first need to leave. That sometimes, to choose our own warmth, we need to feel what it's like without it. She smiled while saying this, tucking a piece of her short auburn hair behind her ear. I sighed along with her.

I left Confidence's home with frangipane on my tongue and her words in my head. I was reminded that she lives in open hearts and uninhibited smiles. And as the sound of my boots clacked against the concrete city streets, I could feel her warm, reassuring hand on mine.

And that was enough.

Excitement

As I walk the bumpy and uneven city sidewalk, my belly is alive; with what, I'm not sure. Words tumble out of my mouth and I don't know what I'm saying. I look down and notice that my shoes are untied and my feet are threatening to come out of them.

Excitement gets the best of me.

I can feel my chest swelling like a mating animal's; the heart inside is manic and quick. If I'm not careful, I'd mistake her for Anxiety. But there's a sweetness about the state of my body, even if it's not one at rest. It feels awake and alive. It feels grounded and safe. Excitement coats my tongue and rings in my ears; I daydream in her revelry.

She finally makes herself known as she rounds a busy street corner. Her buzzed head matches the buzz on my skin. Her dewy cheeks and baby-pink lips match the bubble gum she's chewing; a bubble forms until it pops, her tongue quickly gathering it to chew again. She feels my presence and turns her head to smile. There's that sweetness.

We run to each other, spirited and full. Excitement takes me in her strong arms and hugs me tightly—I feel welcomed, loved, and contained. It's enough to allow my giddy bones to rest, if just for a moment.

We speak quickly but precisely, catching each other up on the happenings of life. We spend our time caught up in being—hours pass, filled in by life, and the sound of a wild human. The presence is thick and warm, yet we move through it with ease. Being with Excitement is akin to Christmas mornings, new lands, old friends, and butterflies in my stomach.

Our days end with a childlike innocence that lingers on our skin and in our bodies; bodies that now seek rest and quiet. We part how we started, with a long embrace and conversation of the next time we will meet, which—surprise, surprise—we can hardly wait for.

I always leave my time with Excitement feeling well fed and clear on what's worth prioritizing in life; what nourishes me, holds me, shows up, and sets my blood on fire.

We turn on opposite street corners with a wink.

She fades into the sky, the girl with the buzzed head and a heart of gold.

I'm boundless with senses abuzz, and I smell of bubble gum.

Playfulness

layfulness and I are steadfast friends.

We visit each other rather often, finding it easiest around birthdays and holidays, celebrations and lazy Sunday nights.

Our gatherings usually consist of light hearts and curious tones.

We always have strawberry jam. And we always eat that strawberry jam by candlelight.

It's our thing.

I like having a thing with Playfulness.

Playfulness has three freckles on her right cheek, which only her closest admirers notice. Her blond banana curls bounce with every giggle that escapes her lips, and her rosemary-colored eyes widen whenever I tell her stories of my past.

She often speaks of the gentleness of a watercolor brushstroke or the uninhibited imagination of children playing. She lives on in the late-night hours, when two lovers keep each other awake with the sound of their laughter or when the ego is put to rest and humor is there to diffuse an argument.

But my favorite part of our visits is the end, when I always notice the hints of strawberry jam on her softly wrinkled blouse.

Workbook Pages for

groovy

STEP 1: GREET

You feel an emotion is present. Say hello and acknowledge that it's here while doing your best not to attach judgment or try to change it, fix it, or remove it. Let it take up space. You can do this. Your body can hold it all.

Now, you can name it. Hello, ... *. Welcome.*

In my body

You feel like . . .

. . . .

. . . .

. . . .

. . . .

. . . .

You taste like . . .

. . . .

. . . .

. . . .

. . . .

. . . .

. . . .

You smell like . . .

. . . .

. . . .

. . . .

. . . .

. . . .

. . . .

You make me want to . . .

. . . .

. . . .

. . . .

. . . .

. . . .

. . . .

As a messenger

You teach me . . .

....
....
....
....
....
....

You show me . . .

....
....
....
....
....
....

You need this to feel seen and heard . . .

....
....
....
....
....
....

Your secret is . . .

. . . .

. . . .

. . . .

. . . .

. . . .

. . . .

. . . .

IF YOU NEED A RAINCHECK:

You need me to make space for you right now, but I don't have the time, accessibility, or availability at the moment. I have a sweet little sun-filled room where you can sit and wait. I'll be back. In the meantime, know that I see you and I'm here to listen.

Time I'll be back:

. . . .

. . . .

. . . .

. . . .

. . . .

. . . .

. . . .

STEP 2: SIT

Hi, it's me. I'm here and ready to sit down to get to know you better. I know you have messages to share and ways to help me grow and heal. Let's sit together and discover the reason for your visit.

What activating event (an experience or a trigger) has currently introduced me to this emotion?

....
....
....
....
....
....

Right after the activating event and before I found myself with this emotion, there's a voice. This can be a belief or a story—something we tell ourselves either out of conditioning or previous experiences. What does this voice or this story say?

....
....
....
....
....
....

How does this story make me feel?

· ·

· ·

· ·

· ·

· ·

· ·

· ·

· ·

· ·

And how does this emotion cause me to react?

· ·

· ·

· ·

· ·

· ·

· ·

· ·

· ·

· ·

How can I honor exactly how I feel? How can I respect what I need most in this moment?

....

....

....

....

....

....

....

....

What is one thing I can do for myself while I'm feeling this emotion that will bring me nourishment? What feels safe here?

....

....

....

....

....

....

....

....

....

STEP 3: CONVERSE

I'm glad we decided to sit down. It may not have been easy or simple, but it created space to understand each other better. It's time for a heart-to-heart.

Time to cue into my senses: Is it cold or warm? Does a breeze blow, or is it humid and thick? What do I feel on my skin when I close my eyes? What do I taste in the air? What smells draw me in? What colors stand out to me?

Where is our meeting place? Am I at my emotion's home, or do we meet somewhere else? Describe the landscape.

....
....
....
....
....
....
....
....
....

What does their home look like? Is their front door ornate or plain? Explain the exterior of their home and what surrounds it.

....
....
....
....
....
....
....
....
....
....

When I step inside their house, what textures do I find? What aesthetic themes emerge? Does it feel warm and cozy or minimalistic and drab? Is there food cooking or the scent of flowers on the table? What stands out to me about stepping into their world?

. . . .

. . . .

. . . .

. . . .

. . . .

. . . .

. . . .

. . . .

When I see the emotion, what does he/she/they look like? What feels striking about them?

. . . .

. . . .

. . . .

. . . .

. . . .

. . . .

. . . .

. . . .

. . . .

What is their disposition? Are they kind? Jovial? Rugged? Quiet?

....

....

....

....

....

....

....

....

....

Do they have a hobby? What do they love to do? What makes them come alive?

....

....

....

....

....

....

....

....

....

What hurts them, scares them, worries them?

What about them surprises me? Speak to their duality.

What stories do they share? What past lives do I learn about? What do they need me to know? Write some dialogue.

. . . .

. . . .

. . . .

. . . .

. . . .

. . . .

. . . .

. . . .

. . . .

. . . .

What is one element about our time together that feels important or stands out?

. . . .

. . . .

. . . .

. . . .

. . . .

. . . .

. . . .

. . . .

. . . .

Is there a shifted perspective and/or physical item(s) I walk away with that reminds me of our time together?

. . . .

. . . .

. . . .

. . . .

. . . .

. . . .

. . . .

. . . .

. . . .

What is this emotion here to tell me?

. . . .

. . . .

. . . .

. . . .

. . . .

. . . .

. . . .

. . . .

. . . .

. . . .

What is one thing I can do right now to help myself and this emotion feel more loved, seen, and accepted?

STEP 4: GRATITUDE AND GOODBYE

I am so grateful for you because you are a part of me. And I am so grateful for me because I am here—growing, committing, and recommitting, messy and disheveled and present. I am a human, and for that I applaud myself. This is my thank-you letter to my emotion and to myself. I acknowledge us for who we are as fully as I can—always holding the easy, the hard, and everything in between.

What insight(s) did I uncover that I'd like to thank my emotion for leading me to?

What part of my emotion and myself am I able to shed a softer light on?

....
....
....
....
....
....
....
....
....

What newfound gratitude do I have for myself and my emotion?

....
....
....
....
....
....
....
....
....

What story was I able to reframe about this emotion?

....
....
....
....
....
....
....
....
....

How does this new thought/perspective make me feel?

....
....
....
....
....
....
....
....
....

When I alchemize/process this emotion, what other supportive emotions do I have access to?

. . . .

. . . .

. . . .

. . . .

. . . .

. . . .

. . . .

. . . .

How has this process shifted the way I react/respond to feeling this emotion, whether toward myself or toward someone else?

. . . .

. . . .

. . . .

. . . .

. . . .

. . . .

. . . .

. . . .

spacious

Tranquil • Peaceful • Grounded

Spacious emotions and full-bodied emotions are second cousins. Where full-bodied emotions take up space in our bodies, spacious emotions create space in our bodies. Often, the all-consuming thunder of meeting with a full-bodied emotion is followed by the deep breath of a spacious emotion. They create space for us to fill our lungs with air and rest our weary bodies for a while. Compassion is a balm for self-criticism. Courage creates a little extra breathing room when things feel heavy, hard, or unknown. These spacious emotions provide shade, comfort, and a feeling of safety and respite. Getting to know them means getting to know what home feels like.

Acceptance

Acceptance tastes bittersweet.

"It's my specialty," she tells me with a smile. "Bittersweet chocolate is the way to go."

I disagree. To be honest, I'm more of a dark chocolate person myself. But I can appreciate the added sweetness of bittersweet chocolate, especially when it's Acceptance who is baking.

She is one of the only people I know who likes to bake in the middle of a desert summer. It's half past noon and her kitchen is sweltering—waves of heat roll from left to right, mimicking the waves in the sand outside.

But she keeps it cool. She can hold space for conflicting, paradoxical natures in a way I admire. She is Acceptance, after all. Hoping for and letting go lives in her bones.

Acceptance lives in an old farmhouse, which sticks out like a sore thumb amid adobe homes. Yet, she's so easy to miss if you aren't sure how to find her, or if you don't want to. Sometimes, I have trouble finding Acceptance's home; there are many times I've walked right by it, willfully ignoring her presence and the smell of baking cookies. I yearn for the solace and wisdom she brings. And on windy, moon-filled nights, I make my way to her home, with dry skin and cracked knuckles. She always lets me in, no matter the time, and she always has something freshly baked. She is nurturing and kind. She loves with her whole heart.

I watch her now—her full, rosy cheeks move from room to room as a welcomed breeze blows the white cotton curtains in time with her body. The pale-yellow kitchen walls have a wallpaper border; the scene of two roosters facing each other with an egg in between them is fitting and quaint, but only in Acceptance's kitchen.

There is always a sense of peace here; a sense that something has been reflected on, thought about, fought with even, and eventually processed. There is a knowing that Acceptance makes her space her own, regardless of what others think. Feelings of resolution and dignity live in her walls, right beside her cuckoo clock.

The sound of a 1950s egg timer goes off, bringing me back to reality, and Acceptance opens up the oven to pull out her chocolate-cinnamon scones. The smell meets my nose, and my mouth instantly salivates.

Acceptance creates an appetite. And more space to move through life. Plus, she was right. Bittersweet chocolate is the way to go.

Contentment

It's the early-morning light that gives Contentment away.

It's not so much the light itself, but the way my husband looks in it, lying next to me. It's the beauty in the routine—the simple way our bodies rest together—that adds meaning to my day. It's how much grace and power they hold; and it's how grand it feels in my bones.

Contentment has a way of making everyday occurrences feel profoundly extraordinary.

I follow the light outside, past the cherry blossoms that are starting to bloom. I hear the tiny yet mighty river speak its lullaby like tongues, and I smile. I often find Contentment meets me in my own backyard on early mornings when the dew stretches across blades of grass and coats my bare feet wet and awake.

I spot her long, dark wavy hair first; it's in a messy bun this morning, with pieces falling around her face, complete with a bright orange bandanna tucking in loose ends. She sits in the grass cross-legged with the innocence of a child and the whimsy of a fairy. It feels so good to see her.

She hears me as I approach and jumps up gleefully to make her way toward me. She has crooked white teeth and plump lips, which she kisses me on the cheek with before pulling me in for a tender hug. The light blue frames of her eyeglasses bump my face as she releases me. She is wonderful.

Contentment has a warmth about her that fills the space and grounds me simultaneously. Like how the soft glow of interior house lights on a spring night make you feel as you walk through your neighborhood—a reminder that gentle, simple moments live inside amid a sometimes sharp and jagged world. Spring gives away the secret of living between worlds; bloom where you're planted and remember warmer days are ahead (and when frost does coat the landscape white, pistachio lattes on cold mornings help).

Contentment and I walk together to her home—past the cherry blossoms, the river, budding trees, and cool morning air. Her sage-colored door greets us along with the smell of freshly made waffles. Her space is anything but perfect; there are dirty dishes in the sink, a shirt hanging on the sofa, and dried-up flowers sitting in a waterless vase. Yet everything feels like it's in its right place. It's in her blood to build a house that feels immediately like a home.

Whenever I enter Contentment's space, I remove my shoes, dig my toes into the plush light-turquoise carpeting, and walk over to a corner of the room where she's set up a space to meditate. She always has visitors meditate upon arriving. She believes it connects us to the present moment, and for Contentment, that's everything. Noticing her current reality—how rich and layered it is—is a way of life for her.

I've got to say, it works. The days I spend at Contentment's are some of my fullest. Her partner, Joy, often emerges from her art studio and takes her place next to Contentment; her legs stretch out on Contentment's lap as she gently moves her hands over Joy's skin. They laugh, tell stories, and reminisce, all while tending to the current moment. I think of you and our early mornings again. I exhale.

Much like Joy, Contentment is a choice. Although not always readily available, she is never hidden. She doesn't play games, she isn't discriminatory. She ebbs and flows, yes. As they all do. But she's willing and ready to reunite when I am. She is a phone call away. She is outside my bedroom door. She is in my loved ones' smiles and in our child's laugh and in the mundane, monotonous moments that make up our days.

When I realize this, I start spending as many days as possible at Contentment's home, collecting these moments and looking at them through her lens. They change color before my eyes, painting themselves bold and bright colors. Psychedelic and alive. They breathe on and on.

And when the antique clock on the wall strikes midnight, I gather my belongings and begin saying my drawn-out goodbyes.

I notice every little thing on my walk back home: the sound of crickets, how the wind moves through the trees, and my own breath. My senses are turned up and turned on.

I remember that soon, the sun will rise.

And I with it.

And then I remember you.

And it's like I never left her home after all.

Humility

On stormy nights, Humility and I meet by the ocean, on the covered white porch that wraps around the back of his house. We listen for the thunder to clap and roll. We watch the lightning flash and strike. We tremble slightly at the large waves that crash hard on the shore below. We sit this way for a while, every so often asking the other, "Did you see that one? Did you feel the earth shake?"

Stormy skies and stormy seas have a way of filling Humility's heart. He says that the natural and raw power they possess reminds him that he's a small part of a much bigger picture.

"Funny," I say back to him, "that's what you do for me."

I remember when I first met Humility. I was fifteen years old. I had scored a game-winning goal against an undefeated team in our field hockey league. I celebrated with my teammates. I celebrated with my parents. And I celebrated every bit of it inside myself, where it felt sacred and seen. The room where Humility and I ate cake and shared feelings felt filling. I remembered thinking, "I like it here."

There was something about Humility's quiet and reserved manner that piqued my interest. For alongside his mild nature was bright, beautiful energy. It was his energy that made me approach him. That and his almond eyes—they held so much and I wanted to know more.

He looked at me knowingly when I walked toward him, like he had been waiting for me. He knew my birthday, my favorite scar, my biggest fear. It felt good to be seen. I smiled up at him, he handed me a piece of cake, and that was that.

I've learned quickly that Humility never denies himself. He never belittles himself or shrinks in size. It's quite the opposite, really. Humility teaches me how to brag—something that, despite popular belief, he's a fan of. The biggest difference is that Humility chooses to see himself and allows that to be enough. He appreciates praise and joyfully shares his wins with others, but he always throws himself a party first—he takes full responsibility in accepting who he is, successes and failures and all. Humility knows he needs to nourish himself first before accepting a piece of cake from someone else.

In the back of his home is a studio filled with a pottery wheel, a kiln, bottles of earth-toned glazes, and lots of pottery tools. Humility loves working with his hands and finds the process of playing with clay to be therapeutic. He believes that whatever energy we're inhabiting comes out in our work. "We rise and we fall," he says. "We become clay in some respect. It's just another form of communication; from vessel to vessel." I tell him that's very poetic. He blows a raspberry at me.

But when I stay and watch Humility mold and cone, center the two-pound ball of clay in front of him, and raise the walls like magic, I see what he means. It's a dance, a movement between him and the clay—an opportunity to mess up or misunderstand at any given point. Humility doesn't care; his ego isn't tied to the earth. His pride and joy for the process alone is enough and it's a part of him, just like the caked-on mud that lines the light switch and doorknobs and everything else he touches as he moves through the room.

Humility gets up and lifts his lidded pot off the wheel. He nods at me and points to where he just sat. "You're up!" he says lovingly. And so I sit down and work hard to center. Mud stays under my nails, and calluses form. The clay underneath moves and wiggles, waiting for me to talk with it. And so, I do. And when I do, it calms, it centers. It opens the door for more mistakes and bigger triumphs, and I realize I'm ready for it all.

So long as Humility is beside me with a piece of cake and his warm eyes.

Clarity

lair de lune by Claude Debussy comes into earshot, and I let out a sigh of relief. Somehow, with just the first few simple piano strokes, my lungs have more space to be. My heart rate slows and my nervous system returns to a simmer. What once felt like boiling water or static noise in my body is quiet and clear.

It's then I see those hazel eyes, and I know.

Clarity is here, and I am so grateful.

His head is full of gorgeous, wavy white hair that was once a dark chestnut brown. I know from an old picture I've seen of him at Peace's home. He reminds me of a young James Taylor. He laughs when I tell him this.

I walk toward him on the beach that's across the street from his home. He likes to meet here. He says that the salty ocean air clears his mind and his sinuses. He tells me that the sand between his toes makes him feel like a kid again. I love Clarity's outlook on life.

We start our walk along the beach deep in conversation, seeing each other in big, bold ways; nodding along in active listening with the occasional "mm-hmm" or "yes!" After some time though, we settle into our rhythm and walk in silence while collecting sand dollars and placing them carefully in the handwoven basket Clarity brings with him specifically for this purpose.

Clarity has sand dollars lining the shelves in his home. Some broken, some full, all of them carefully cleaned and placed gently in their rightful place. He gifts them to people when they're feeling out of sorts or are ruminating. He likes how taking the time to patiently wipe away the sand reveals new lines and shapes. He likes how within each sand dollar lives layers of stories and insights—all waiting to be found.

I notice that I visit Clarity after moments of confusion, inner turmoil, or frustration. Sometimes, my stays are brief, sometimes they're extended, but with Clarity, it has always been quality over quantity. He hits hard and nourishes quickly, like homemade chicken soup or dark chocolate.

On one of my visits, I asked him about Peace and how they met. He smiled that smile he usually reserves for her and looked into my eyes.

"Peace," he said, "keeps me alive in the moment. I value that. I feel most like myself when I can focus in and ground down, one moment at a time. Those moments add up to something. They add up to a life." He cleared his throat and continued. "But Peace has also taught me that being clear in each moment isn't always an option. And that's okay. She's still there with me. We're still together. I can find her as I wander. That's clarity in and of itself. It's clarity of the heart."

Clarity is not about having it all figured out. Clarity is about seeing your hand in front of you and trusting that it's yours; even when it's foggy and dark, and the shapes blur and twist. Clarity is about knowing you'll see your hand again, and no matter what it looks like or how it's changed, it's still a part of you. When I embody Clarity, I know that whatever comes next—hard or easy, scary or safe—I'll gain newfound insight and wisdom, and because of that, I'll never be lost.

Eventually, the wind whips and the waves spray, and Clarity and I walk back across the street to his home, where we're greeted with home-made cinnamon buns. I sit down and do sudoku with him—which, in reality, is me watching him do it—and savor the way his wrinkled hand hovers over each box until he knows what to write down next. I adore the way his tongue hangs ever so slightly out of his mouth as he concentrates. But what I love most of all is the way he trusts himself, for every line and swoop—every number that fills the space—is done in pen. And there is nothing but peace surrounding us both.

Courage

Courage is warm to the touch. Her gray hair is short and straight, her dark-brown eyes are soothing. She reminds me of Mrs. Claus, jolly and grounded. She reminds me of what it feels like to be scared and to show up anyway.

Courage always shows up. Without fail, she is there with her comforting touch, a hand-knit shawl, and an embrace that steadies whatever part of my body is still shaking.

I like arriving at Courage's. The inside of her home is full of textures—wool, satin, and antique woods. It boasts jewel tones and feels rich and inviting. My personal favorite is her deep-teal velvet couch. It's here that I place myself when I enter Courage's space—in deep need of her steady hand and warm chamomile tea.

Outside, big oak trees line her property, and at night, the wind through the leaves feels peaceful and calming. It's a much-appreciated reprieve from recent nights that seem far too still for comfort.

My time at Courage's varies from big happenings to small gatherings, long visits to short stays. Sometimes, I call on Courage in last-minute moments with panic in my voice and fear in my heart. Other times, I pull on Courage's gravitational force for long, extended stretches; her stamina and endurance are two things I lean heavily on her for.

Regardless of their length, our visits are quality, and they fill me with wisdom and experience. They humble me. But most importantly, they are filled with endless amounts of love.

It's in the incredibly tender moments—birth and death, loss and uncharted territory, new houses and old wounds, hellos and goodbyes—that Courage shows up with love in tow. Without love, Courage is cool to the touch. She's pure logic, a means of pushing through. She's a shell of herself.

It's the love—held by Courage's body and perpetually rosy cheeks—that makes it possible to move through fear, despair, and the unknown. It's love that makes navigating fear so worthy.

Through Courage, I've learned that being brave means being myself—imperfect, messy, unwound, and unkind at times. She does not judge. She wouldn't dare. She understands what it means to be human. She understands that being human is the most courageous thing we do.

And in being human, there are times I feel scared she won't show up; times I'm nervous I won't know her if I see her. There are times I worry that I'll sit on her soft velvet couch with nothing to say.

But without fail, she's there. Without fail, her short gray hair falls in straight lines and her dark-brown eyes offer strength and support.

She reaches out with a warm touch and a blanket over my shoulders. She delivers hot tea.

And when I'm ready to hear it, she sits down next to me with her hand on mine.

"You are here," she whispers, "and that's enough."

Grounded

Whenever I meet with Grounded, I lose my shoes. It's like they walk away on their own, perhaps scavenging about for clarity and purpose. Sometimes, I wonder if they've found what they're looking for. Sometimes, they come back to me muddied and tired.

All I know is that when I'm with Grounded, clarity and purpose find me—barefoot yet present.

Grounded lives on a hilly, heavily wooded piece of land that backs up to an even denser forest. No matter the time of year, the trees dress up. Bright reds and deep oranges fill the landscape during autumn, and in winter, the snow covers everything in white; peaceful and still. Spring is quiet and bare, flirty in nature with budding flowers and leaves. And summer is lush; humidity dances in the air and asks you to lie down with it, if just for a while. It's a true haven.

He's carved walking trails through five of the thirteen acres and walks them daily. He insists that we walk them barefoot. He insists that the earth is good for the soul and the skin. And when Grounded insists on something, I trust him.

On weekends, his young daughter joins us and together we collect dandelions, chase bunnies, and lie down in the grass. She amplifies his energy. And he loves her up.

The thing that I've come to learn from my time with Grounded is how simple it all is. In certain moments and around certain people, I strive to be accepted, to belong. But when I'm with Grounded, all that matters is being. Not who I'm being, what I'm being, or when. Just that I'm there in the moment, belonging to myself until everything else around me comes into focus.

Grounded is handsome, with dark-brown hair and laugh lines. He rubs his stubble when he speaks, especially about something deep or revealing. He's earnest about his hopes and fears. He speaks openly about his missteps and failures. And on late nights when the heat hangs in the air and lightning bugs make their debut like stars on Earth, Grounded shares his insecurities and shortcomings.

What I find most insightful is how even in these moments, Grounded never falters from his sense of self. He simply laughs into the night air, looks down with his blue eyes, which show lines of deep yellow and green, and exhales. He embraces the nuanced imperfections of being human.

And he speaks of it all with grace, compassion, and love.

He speaks of it all with his two bare feet planted firmly on the ground.

When I leave Grounded's home, I gather my belongings, which now consist of one less pair of shoes, but I never end up missing them anyway.

Where there is ground beneath my feet, there is life.

And he lives on.

Forgiveness

In the forest town where Forgiveness lives, she is known as the "miracle maker."

People flock to her from all over, pleading, yearning, begging to understand how everything she touches is love. Forgiveness doesn't say much. She doesn't need to, for she speaks through her actions. But when she does speak, she speaks only of miracles.

She tells us that miracles can happen in a split second.

A change of circumstance. A change in scenery.

And the biggest miracle of all, a change of heart.

"There," she explains, "is where I live."

Forgiveness also physically lives in the forest, although she's wandered nomadically most of her life. She serves the people, and that means meeting others where they are.

Her house is simple and functional, with little decor or artwork on the walls. In this sense, it feels spacious and inviting, like her one-room home is full of endless possibility. Everything feels easier as I sit down on her Moroccan floor pillow—my breath, my thoughts, my wounds. I rest for the first time in a long while, happy to hand over my fight-or-flight response, which Forgiveness so generously takes from me.

She keeps very few personal belongings, which makes me all the more intrigued with what she does have in her home. A ceramic teapot with deep blues and yellows sits on her stove next to a porcelain vase filled with dried sunflowers. She has journal after journal stacked up against her large-paned window that looks out over grassland and deep forest. Her house smells of cardamom, and an off-white, hand-knit blanket sits gently on the back of an antique oak chair. As I turn to face the room again, I realize that Forgiveness's home is one of the most welcoming spaces I've ever ventured into.

And yet, there are still times I sit on Forgiveness's stoop, willing myself to walk in. Meeting with Forgiveness is a practice. The longer I stay away, the quicker she fades from my existence. But on warm spring nights when everyone ventures out of their homes to smile at strangers on the street with hope on their lips, you can feel Forgiveness.

In moments when wounded pride and ego soften like honey as it meets milk, you can see Forgiveness.

And when you look into the eyes of someone you love and see them shining back, warm and willing to receive all we are and aren't, you can choose Forgiveness.

It's only then I feel her rush my body, hold my hands in hers, and whisper gently, "*You* are the miracle."

Peace

Peace is an older woman with a beautiful long white-and-gray braid of hair that runs down the side of her face and rests on her shoulder. A few baby-pink strands wrap themselves in and out, like a child jumping double Dutch. Whenever I meet with Peace, I reflect on how fitting this is; how she is forever a streak of cool color in a gray world.

Today, I meet Peace by the river, behind her forest home. She's in the middle of her Tai Chi practice. I make sure to enter her space slowly and carefully, so I can catch a glimpse of her in movement. My heart rate slows, and my cells begin to match those of the forest's. Catching Peace in her element feels akin to watching a wild animal walk proudly and confidently through its land.

Peace is groovy; she loves the Bee Gees and Willie Nelson and usually puts on one of their records while she sautés mushrooms in truffle oil alongside scrambled eggs and a cup of ginger tea. She moves to and fro, swaying her hips in rhythm with the song, occasionally singing a few words from the handful of lines she knows by heart.

Peace's is a place I never want to leave.

While Peace cooks, I walk freely around her home gazing at black-and-white pictures of people I've met before. There's an image of her arm around Acceptance's neck, the two of them caught with wide grins on their faces. "My sister," she says, turning around to notice me. I nod. That makes total sense.

Next, I see a well-loved yarn bracelet tied to Peace's keys and reach to pick it up. "Compassion made me that when she was a kid," she says, smiling. "My sweet girl."

But my favorite picture of all is the one with her and Clarity. His hazel eyes sparkle as he looks at Peace, who is much younger than she is now. It's fascinating to see her in all her glory as a young woman, and heart-warming to see how much she's stayed the same. Her smile is big and uninhibited, as though caught in the middle of a laugh. Her nature is grounding and warm. And her hand is clasped in Clarity's, who has wrapped his whole arm around her waist and is actively pulling her closer. I look up and catch Peace's expression. She needn't say more; their love is written all over her face.

At night, when I return home, I journal about our time together. I write:

1. Peace is universal and can look different depending on the person, the season, and the situation.
2. Although at times the road is challenging, we can find our way to Peace.
3. There are methods that help me find her, like deep breaths, advocating for my needs, and acceptance.

4. She is in the trees and the sound that snow makes.

5. Peace helps me center and expand so that I can see the rest of the picture—the corners come into view like a folded-back photo. Something was missing, and it was her, even though she never really left.

That last part resonates throughout my body, and I close my eyes. It's there that I see her—the swaying of the trees matches the swaying of her body—and I fall asleep to the image of Peace dancing away under tall redwoods.

Gratitude

Gratitude is a homebody.

If you ask her, she'll invite you in.

She'll make English tea, warm up brown bread, and pull the strawberry rhubarb jam from the freezer. She'll put on a fire if it's cool or open the windows if it's warm. She has a way of making the simplest of everyday movements feel intentional, comforting, and special.

Gratitude has a garden.

If you ask her, she'll tell you about it.

She'll take you through her process, she'll share her gardening secrets, and she'll even tell you about her favorite plants—something she usually reserves for your third or fourth visit. She's careful not to play favorites in front of them. She knows how attentively they listen.

Gratitude's light is always on.

If you ask her, she'll leave it that way. Over the course of our time together, I've learned how important my relationship with Gratitude is. She's a giver and a knower. And she, too, yearns for a reciprocal love.

So now, when I'm walking home, I try to always stop at Gratitude's. She packs me a basket of brown bread. She fills a glass jar with strawberry rhubarb jam. She hands me a rose (her favorite flower). And although the visit may be quick, the nourishment is deep.

Gratitude moves with love.

And if you ask her to walk you home, she'll take your hand in hers and lead the way.

Compassion

ompassion's beauty is felt before she enters the room.

She stands out in a crowd, with her long, dark wavy hair and warm skin. I remember when we first met. She took my hand in hers and began to read my palm, her catlike eyes meeting mine with each explanation of the lines my hand held.

I remember the bluish-green veins on her wrists and arms.

And how infinite I felt.

Compassion sits well in silence. Her happy place is any space she can sit and really listen to someone else. Small coffee shops, dimly lit bookstores, intimate living rooms. She's always encouraging others to join her. And more often than not, they do.

I can feel her radiance grow when others are around; she lives for helping connect people to their true nature.

She believes her purpose in this world is to walk us all home.

Her home is a small bungalow nestled amid pine trees. It boasts floor-to-ceiling windows, as though to invite the outside in, and at night you can hear cricket symphonies laced with the mellow bass of frogs joining in. Coyotes yelp, and the whole natural world comes alive. But that's what Compassion does. She revives and nurtures everything around her. The forest is no exception.

When the sky becomes a twilight blue and the stars reveal themselves ever so slowly, like freckles after a long summer, Compassion pulls out her ukulele and sings. Her favorite songs are by Maggie Rogers, although she also loves "I've Seen All Good People" by the band Yes. Her voice carries into the night, and for a moment, I forget where I am. I linger in the air for a while with the quiet, the mist, and a feeling of acceptance and profound love.

There was one night in particular that I arrived at Compassion's door—lightning lit up the sky and thunder roared. I was soaked through and through. It was late, but Compassion answered the door in her silky bathrobe, her eye mask covering one eye and the rest pulled halfway up her forehead. When she saw it was me, she quickly unlocked the door and held me. I slumped into her arms and cried.

I had spent the last few weeks at Grief's home after a loss that rocked my heart off-balance. The first few days we spent together, I could not escape the shame and blame I carried with me. They held fast to me, like a breastfeeding child, and I sunk deeper into darkness. They needed me in that moment. And I was okay with that. But after a few days together, they were ready to part. It was I who now held them close with white knuckles and an unsteady breath.

Grief saw this and suggested I see Compassion. And so I did.

The night I arrived, Compassion put on tea water and lit tapered candles. We sat in her kitchen at an antique ebony table and said nothing for a while.

Like I said, Compassion sits well in silence.

Once I began to dry off and the night settled deeper into my skin, Compassion looked up at me and asked quietly, "What do you need?" I spoke to her about my self-criticism; the ways in which I wasn't enough. The ways in which I wasn't worthy and how my flaws and mistakes made me obsolete, undeserving of forgiveness or love.

She took her hand in mine again and spoke of a space where freedom, love, and tenderness exist. A space that no one can alter. A home inside that no matter the weather, the floors are dry, the bed is warm, and joy lives within the walls. A true haven of acceptance, in all circumstances.

"That," she whispered, "is self-compassion. I am as much for you as I am for me. You need to nurture yourself the same way you nurture others. If we hold ourselves to such a harsh way of being, we hold others to the same."

I slept soundly that night, sharing a bed with Compassion. And when I left in the morning, she watched me from her floor-to-ceiling windows in her silky robe and messy hair and waved until I was out of sight.

I will continue to meet with Compassion for the rest of my life, grateful for every minute we spend together. With each visit, I take one step closer to home.

And the lines on my hands tell the way.

Workbook Pages for
spacious

STEP 1: GREET

You feel an emotion is present. Say hello and acknowledge that it's here while doing your best not to attach judgment or try to change it, fix it, or remove it. Let it take up space. You can do this. Your body can hold it all.

Now, you can name it. Hello, ... Welcome.

In my body

You feel like . . .

. . . .

. . . .

. . . .

. . . .

. . . .

You taste like . . .

....
....
....
....
....
....

You smell like . . .

....
....
....
....
....
....

You make me want to . . .

....
....
....
....
....
....
....

As a messenger

You teach me . . .

....
....
....
....
....
....

You show me . . .

....
....
....
....
....
....

You need this to feel seen and heard . . .

....
....
....
....
....
....

Your secret is . . .

....
....
....
....
....
....
....

IF YOU NEED A RAINCHECK:

You need me to make space for you right now, but I don't have the time, accessibility, or availability at the moment. I have a sweet little sun-filled room where you can sit and wait. I'll be back. In the meantime, know that I see you and I'm here to listen.

Time I'll be back:

....
....
....
....
....
....
....

STEP 2: SIT

Hi, it's me. I'm here and ready to sit down to get to know you better. I know you have messages to share and ways to help me grow and heal. Let's sit together and discover the reason for your visit.

What activating event (an experience or a trigger) has currently introduced me to this emotion?

. . . .

. . . .

. . . .

. . . .

. . . .

. . . .

Right after the activating event and before I found myself with this emotion, there's a voice. This can be a belief or a story—something we tell ourselves either out of conditioning or previous experiences. What does this voice or this story say?

. . . .

. . . .

. . . .

. . . .

. . . .

. . . .

How does this story make me feel?

. . . .

. . . .

. . . .

. . . .

. . . .

. . . .

. . . .

. . . .

. . . .

And how does this emotion cause me to react?

. . . .

. . . .

. . . .

. . . .

. . . .

. . . .

. . . .

. . . .

. . . .

How can I honor exactly how I feel? How can I respect what I need most in this moment?

. . . .

. . . .

. . . .

. . . .

. . . .

. . . .

. . . .

. . . .

What is one thing I can do for myself while I'm feeling this emotion that will bring me nourishment? What feels safe here?

. . . .

. . . .

. . . .

. . . .

. . . .

. . . .

. . . .

. . . .

. . . .

STEP 3: CONVERSE

I'm glad we decided to sit down. It may not have been easy or simple, but it created space to understand each other better. It's time for a heart-to-heart.

Time to cue into my senses: Is it cold or warm? Does a breeze blow, or is it humid and thick? What do I feel on my skin when I close my eyes? What do I taste in the air? What smells draw me in? What colors stand out to me?

Where is our meeting place? Am I at my emotion's home, or do we meet somewhere else? Describe the landscape.

....

....

....

....

....

....

....

....

What does their home look like? Is their front door ornate or plain? Explain the exterior of their home and what surrounds it.

....

....

....

....

....

....

....

....

....

....

When I step inside their house, what textures do I find? What aesthetic themes emerge? Does it feel warm and cozy or minimalistic and drab? Is there food cooking or the scent of flowers on the table? What stands out to me about stepping into their world?

. . . .

. . . .

. . . .

. . . .

. . . .

. . . .

. . . .

When I see the emotion, what does he/she/they look like? What feels striking about them?

. . . .

. . . .

. . . .

. . . .

. . . .

. . . .

. . . .

. . . .

What is their disposition? Are they kind? Jovial? Rugged? Quiet?

. . . .

. . . .

. . . .

. . . .

. . . .

. . . .

. . . .

. . . .

. . . .

. . . .

Do they have a hobby? What do they love to do? What makes them come alive?

. . . .

. . . .

. . . .

. . . .

. . . .

. . . .

. . . .

. . . .

. . . .

What hurts them, scares them, worries them?

What about them surprises me? Speak to their duality.

What stories do they share? What past lives do I learn about? What do they need me to know? Write some dialogue.

....

....

....

....

....

....

....

....

....

....

What is one element about our time together that feels important or stands out?

....

....

....

....

....

....

....

....

....

Is there a shifted perspective and/or physical item(s) I walk away with that reminds me of our time together?

. . . .

. . . .

. . . .

. . . .

. . . .

. . . .

. . . .

. . . .

. . . .

. . . .

What is this emotion here to tell me?

. . . .

. . . .

. . . .

. . . .

. . . .

. . . .

. . . .

. . . .

. . . .

. . . .

What is one thing I can do right now to help myself and this emotion feel more loved, seen, and accepted?

STEP 4: GRATITUDE AND GOODBYE

I am so grateful for you because you are a part of me. And I am so grateful for me because I am here—growing, committing, and recommitting, messy and disheveled and present. I am a human, and for that I applaud myself. This is my thank-you letter to my emotion and to myself. I acknowledge us for who we are as fully as I can—always holding the easy, the hard, and everything in between.

What insight(s) did I uncover that I'd like to thank my emotion for leading me to?

. . . .

. . . .

. . . .

. . . .

. . . .

. . . .

. . . .

. . . .

. . . .

. . . .

. . . .

. . . .

. . . .

. . . .

What part of my emotion and myself am I able to shed a softer light on?

....
....
....
....
....
....
....
....
....

What newfound gratitude do I have for myself and my emotion?

....
....
....
....
....
....
....
....
....
....

What story was I able to reframe about this emotion?

....

....

....

....

....

....

....

....

....

....

How does this new thought/perspective make me feel?

....

....

....

....

....

....

....

....

....

....

When I alchemize/process this emotion, what other supportive emotions do I have access to?

. . . .

. . . .

. . . .

. . . .

. . . .

. . . .

. . . .

. . . .

. . . .

How has this process shifted the way I react/respond to feeling this emotion, whether toward myself or toward someone else?

. . . .

. . . .

. . . .

. . . .

. . . .

. . . .

. . . .

. . . .

. . . .

. . . .

transcendent

Expansive · Interconnected · Spiritual

Transcendent emotions create a sense of interconnect-
edness—to the universe, nature, the collective, our inner
selves. They're good indicators of what people, activities,
and experiences open our minds and remind us that
we're "spiritual beings having a human experience."
When do you find yourself feeling connected with something bigger or someone outside yourself? How does this
affect the way you view yourself in relationship to the
world around you?

Awe

we is a healer.

He's creative, miraculous, and unassuming. He touches all kinds of beings: those who know him well and those who are still seeking.

We all know him by the way our mouths hang open as wonder floods our bodies, often when we're around nature or children, and when time slows down.

But what no one knows about Awe is his love for popcorn and sour gummy worms.

I know this because it's what I bring him every time we meet.

And every time, he sits cross-legged on the dirt underneath the sky-lit night and sighs.

"This," he says between each bite, ". . . this is where it's at."

I meet Awe in the desert at night because it's when his shift begins. We usually set up camp as the sun sets, and vivid shades of pink, terra-cotta, and cobalt soak the sky, thanks to the dry air. We place folding chairs around a fire while we share a canteen of fresh water. I smack my lips as Awe begins popping popcorn over the fire. He takes a quick break and steals a sip of gin from his flask as the air gets colder.

Pretty soon, the sun has hung up his hat, and Awe and I are content, with full bellies. He looks at his watch, and when he closes his eyes and begins to listen, I know it's time.

We walk slowly to a row of white flowers and wait. Awe explains that these saguaro cacti bloom for only one day of the year, and at night, they attract lesser long-nosed bats and Mexican long-tongued bats for pollination. The cacti themselves can grow up to fifty feet or more while the flowers that grow at the end of their arms will only reach about three inches in diameter. And the bright-red, juicy fruit they produce smells of overripe melon.

This relationship, although short-lived, is pure magic. And it's Awe who holds the space and sets the scene.

I watch as white petals open gracefully and with ease; I see bats respond to their call and drink nectar from flowers that are now fully bloomed in the moonlight. I stand still as nature, in all her glory, dances with Awe in a slow, sensual bolero-style dance, and when I close my eyes, I can feel healing everywhere.

We walk back home barefoot; the sand is cool and soft without the heat of the sun. We don't say much—we don't need to; the silence holds a container for the beauty and ethereality still moving through our bodies.

When we reach the dark wooden door of his desert bungalow, I say goodbye to Awe with a hug. We talk excitedly about our next meeting, and he thanks me for the popcorn and sour gummy worms. I thank him for the out-of-this-world experience.

I turn back slowly from where we came, watching the flowers slowly close. And just like that, Awe is gone.

But only in physical form.

There is a faith in something much bigger than me that lingers in my chest cavity.

Awe is a healer.

Hope

Hope smells of honeysuckle, and her lips are always full of color. She drives a dusty matte-yellow VW van and has forever called the ocean home. Sometimes, she yearns for the darkness of the desert. She tells me that at night, the stars gossip, and it helps put her to sleep.

She gravitates toward guitar solos and acoustic melodies, but every now and then, she'll throw on a metal song from the early 2000s and rock out. I can see the inhibitions fly off her with each headbang, and in a subtle way, I feel my own body soften into the worn-in leather seats.

What I always notice about my time with Hope is that she lives in a state of perpetual trust. Trust in people. Trust in goodness. Trust in herself. One night around a boasting fire, I asked her how she found that deep knowing within. I noticed the fire reflect in her light-brown eyes and saw her body shudder.

Hope told me of a story of Despair. A relationship that consumed her and left her doubled over from the pain. A cocktail laced with fear, sadness, and rage. It wasn't Despair's fault; they found their way there together. And as they sat licking their wounds, pulling pieces of glass from their skin and drinking honey to soothe their throats coarse from screaming, they joined hands. And they chose.

They chose a new dream. A new reality. A new future. And soon, that vision became so clear, they were able to stand. The next day, they took a step. And soon after that, another. When they emerged from their time in the under- and inner world, they saw themselves. They weren't the same as when they entered, but they knew they were closer to their truths than ever before. For the first time in their lives, they understood what they needed to do to keep walking toward the future they had dreamed up together.

Amid the pain and the fear and the aching, Hope lives. And so do we.

A groovy song comes on over the small travel speaker, and Hope drops her earth-covered blanket to the ground as she stands up and begins to move.

I swear I see the stars come down to meet her. And as they seem to melt toward her softened face, I watch her whisper back, "Soon. I'm on my way."

Love

Love is known for her twenty-twenty vision.

She spots a friend from across the street and runs to them with open arms long before they look up from their phone and realize she's standing in front of them. She sees life so clearly; I often envy her.

But on warm spring days when the sun is high in the sky and the air is heavier than it has been in months, I spot her on an empty street where she colors every step she takes and slowly brings every person she passes to life.

And I'm so grateful she exists.

She is the most expansive person I have ever met, able to hold space internally for conflicting ideas, beliefs, and ways of being. Nothing is ever black-and-white with her. It isn't even gray. It is the ultimate rainbow, a spectrum for sore eyes. She's heart-centered and full-bodied, and the older I get, the more I realize she's the ultimate truth; the answer to why I am here.

Love lives in a small and magical hand-built studio on an acre of land in a small woodsy town. Her lover built it for her when she was in a time of transformation, filling in the internal spaces she inhabited like clay fills the hands that shape it. She nests there with her lover, their dog, and a row of sunflowers out front. The studio is mostly windows, with stained sidings and white trim. It's free-spirited yet grounding in every way. It's home.

We spend many days sitting here, breaking apart Oreos and dipping them in peanut butter. Usually, we talk the day away about things that move us; things that bring us to tears or to someone else's arms. And when the night gets cool and that heaviness in the air lifts, we talk about heartbreak.

The shards of our broken selves glimmer in the moonlight as we hold them in our hands for the other person to examine, acknowledge, and appreciate. On nights when we stay up late, we talk about why we want to love at all when it exposes us, leaves us raw, and can hurt to the very depths of our being.

But we always come back to the same point: that a life without Love is not a life at all.

And that a life with Love is possible for every single being.

She speaks softly to the humans whose hearts yearn to beat alongside others', those who understand the risk of loving and still see value in it.

The people who find Love healing, soothing, a balm for the human experience.

And to the soulful, who keep choosing to accept themselves and others no matter the outcome, no matter how messy.

That is the Love I know. And I can say with every cell in my body that I never want to live a day without her by my side.

So, there I lie, next to her. We become quiet, nothing but our breath to fill the space. I close my eyes and call it in, overcome with so much. Reminded that my body can hold it all.

Without her, I don't exist.

I've never felt so at home as I do in Love's house.

Wonder

I met Wonder in the forest as a child.

I had followed a deer to his house over the train tracks and found his earth-toned cottage nestled deep among the brush. On the way, I passed forts constructed of decaying trees and broken-off branches. The air was soft, dewy, and sweet. And the only thing that walked with me was the sound of my feet against the forest floor, the train horn as it rode alongside me, and the soft patter of deer hooves that led the way.

I continued to visit him most of my childhood—usually on Thursdays, when my parents worked late. Wonder cooked a mean stew.

His place was an oasis: warm, cozy, and inviting. I was far from home, a thought that would normally agitate me, but at Wonder's I felt safe. There was so much to explore there—an old Scrabble board in the corner of the room, a well-loved tire swing under his favorite tree, a cast-iron stove that warmed the entire space, and a row of roses that lined the back fence of his property.

I always knew I was getting close by the hazy smell of rose that emanated from his windows. One day I asked him about it.

He lit his pipe, inhaled deeply, closed his dark-brown eyes, and waved his hand in the air as though he were painting the image in his mind on his bare white walls. "People called her Beauty," he said.

"I was a child when I met her, right here in this forest. My eyes were just being opened to the world. Her eyes, it seemed, had been opened from the first moment she arrived. She was an old soul, a good listener. She was kind. She was my first friend.

"A deer led me to her as well. The soft white spots on its back caught my attention. The sound of the wind through the crispy fall leaves cheered me on. When I first saw Beauty, her cheeks were rosy from the cool afternoon air and her smile was big. She was expansive; talking to her was like having a conversation with God herself. Before I left, she leaned in and whispered something in my ear. It tickled and I laughed."

I watched his lips curl up and his eyes soften as he continued: "She told me to always plant roses. It didn't matter what color or how many as long as they were planted in a place where I dwelled—a place that I'd see daily. She carried rose petals in her pocket wherever she roamed, to remind her how something so complex and delicate can be so wondrous. She told me that they were humble flowers, finding joy in simply being. She taught me how to slow down and notice. Now it's a way of life. I have her to thank."

I hugged the quilt around my shoulders a bit tighter, imagining Beauty as I soaked up the smell of rose into my cells.

Oh, what a person you must be, I thought, to cause Wonder to open his brown eyes that much wider.

Kindness

indness is exactly how you'd think she'd be—unassuming, gentle, and simple. She just is. She wears no air of expectation or judgment. She never keeps score or manipulates a situation to get what she wants.

She stands in her olive skin the way the sun lives in the sky—boldly and generously.

It was the boldness that caught my attention. Don't get me wrong, Kindness is sweet, but she's fierce in nature. She isn't afraid to show up; a soft smile, an extended hand, an intentional and focused attention. She wears herself on her sleeve and she never worries that it will dirty, scratch, or stain.

There are people who mock her or, in some cases, fear her. They make assumptions that she's up to something—something they can't quite see or understand.

But I know Kindness enough to know that isn't the case. What you see is what you get. It's the most incredible thing about her.

Kindness lives in a small colonial-style home, painted a deep blue-green with rust-colored shutters and a white porch in the front. She has daffodils lining the walkway to her very-light-pink front door. She gathers them on Fridays and arranges them in glass vases and ceramic pitchers; she likes having fresh blooms to welcome her on weekend mornings.

Kindness knows how to save parts of herself for herself—a tip that she gave me as I grew older. "Boundaries are important," she said. "Without self-respect and love, I can't be me."

I nodded, reflecting on times Kindness would show up late to our meetings, burnt out. She'd sleep for what seemed like a week before waking up and smiling at me through tired eyes. Or moments when Kindness would be met with hate or fear. I'd watch her cower at first, but with time and reflection, she would sit herself back up, smooth out her gingham dress, and try again.

She understands better than anyone I know that we need to meet people where they're at without judging the footsteps that got them there or what way they choose to go afterward.

It's why she sweeps each night; to even the road we walk and clear the air for visitors.

I love being a visitor in Kindness's home. We're old friends who often talk over homemade lemonade, complete with a cayenne-salted rim. I notice how life changes when I don't frequent Kindness's home, and I feel more like myself inside her four walls than most other places.

Now, Kindness has a bed laid out for me and a space to call my own, with a typewriter in the corner overlooking the daffodils that line her walkway.

And some weekend mornings, I sit up in bed and watch her sweep, as she prepares for the next soul who needs her.

Sensuality

strum a guitar, slowly and smoothly. Its hum fills the room, and textures begin to dance.

The oatmeal-colored fur blanket.

The blossom of a tea candle nearby.

The thickness of sandalwood in the air.

Their raspy voice comes into focus and I bite my lip.

I have it bad for Sensuality.

"I have a reputation," they say, as they play with one of their locs, "for being purely sexual. But I exist in other places, too."

I understand what Sensuality is talking about. I feel them often in my skin when I've been playing under the sun. The way velvet feels on my fingertips. The way music sounds on drunk ears.

The truth is, Sensuality and I hang out quite a lot despite how taboo people try to make them. I love that they're bold. They wear it proudly, and that soul-deep acceptance turns me on. Being with them feels so easy. We usually light a joint, play records, and talk on the cloudlike pillows that make tiny villages on the floor of their home. It's here I often find myself giddy, open-hearted, and wrapped in ecstasy until the early morning.

"You see," they continue, "I live in those in-between moments when you feel an experience with your whole body. Your hairs stand on end, your lips curl up, and you completely surrender. Moments where you can close your eyes and smell the salt in the air. Taste it on your skin. Come alive from the inside out."

It's they who taught me how soft lips and heavy breathing feel wild and precious simultaneously.

As the sun rises, I help Sensuality clean dishes—us in our usual positions of them washing and me drying—and say goodbye with a lingering embrace.

Forever walking away with the smell of sandalwood in my hair.

Curiosity

What if curiosity didn't kill the cat?

What if it made the cat a more expansive, open-eyed creature? What if that cat explored a new city, learned a new language, or took up with a lover?

What if people thought curiosity killed the cat because they no longer recognized it?

Or what if curiosity did kill the cat, but not in the way we're taught to think? What if curiosity killed an outdated version of the cat and allowed the cat to awake fully to a more authentic, grounded, bold version of itself?

What if curiosity actually *gave* the cat life?

These are the conversations Curiosity and I have as we sit on his mauve-colored cushions; the groovy light from the lava lamp in the corner paints our skin a faint orange and pale pink. We share passion fruit by passing a plate of small, purple, seedy bulbs between us and eat the fleshy, sweet insides with a spoon.

"I am much more than a gateway to mischief," he explains as his honey-brown eyes smile, revealing soft wrinkles I want to reach out and touch. "I'm the gateway to an open mind."

I know this to be true of Curiosity.

He's the one who leads me away from judgment and back to his arms. He's always warm to the touch. He keeps me humble. And he values learning over knowing. He steers me in the direction of life—things, people, and places that expand my way of thinking—and he sits with me while I ask, "Why this? Why here? Why now?"

Curiosity is the lover of Possibility, the two of them bringing the world aglow with their energy; like seeing through the eyes of an acid trip.

Or a child.

Today, I sit with Curiosity in his home and we discuss dreams and plans, musings and wonders.

Eventually, we move from cushions to cloud watching, both of us content as we lie on a grassy knoll just beyond Curiosity's home. I share that I'm curious about what my baby's favorite color will be, curious about what strangers I'll lock eyes with tomorrow and how I can be more flexible, more loving. Curious at who I'm evolving into with every second and every breath and every turn of the sun.

The afternoon passes, and Curiosity sinks deeper into the grass below him, runs his fingers through his dark hair, and looks at me with a smile. It's time to go home.

But the truth about Curiosity is that he's everywhere.

He follows me home in the way the trees move during a summer storm. He greets me as I watch bees fly hurriedly from one bloom to the next. He falls asleep with me when self-judgment and fear arise with the dimming light and growing night. When I wake up, he is nowhere to be seen, but the question "What else is possible?" is on my lips.

A soft smile on my face.

And the taste of passion fruit in my mouth.

Vulnerability

There is an ocean outside Vulnerability's home that I visit often. Most times, it's warm and inviting. It's steady and still. But in colder months, it's icy and wild; stepping into it feels jarring and unnerving. I've learned to love those initial pangs of cold, for I know the farther out I wade, the warmer and calmer it gets. And on nights when the moon is big and bright in the mosaic-like sky, I walk down to the shore, remove every single piece of clothing, and dive in.

This purging before meeting Vulnerability has become a sort of ritual for us. I spend my time quietly floating on the buoyant water, held by the salty air and the tides. The moon reaches down with her glow and bathes me in light. And I slowly inhale.

Meeting Vulnerability requires deep breaths.

I walk out of the water with the sea-foam stuck to my legs like bubbles in a bath. My towel is dry from the night air, my clothes gathered in a pile like animals huddled together to stay warm. I scoop them up and walk quietly and carefully up the sandy dirt path that leads to Vulnerability's.

Vulnerability's home is a sweet, quaint cottage by the sea in the company of wind-blown trees. They're miscolored and misshapen from years of putting themselves out there—years living amid the elements. They're bare and bruised. But they're also incredibly strong, grounded, and happy in their skin. They wave to me as I walk by.

His terra-cotta walkway is surrounded by dusty millers just starting to bloom—the yellow flowers bashfully stretching their arms out toward the sky in conversation. I find my feet know the way, even when I don't. They step intentionally on broken slabs of terra-cotta so that one side of the slab is lifted and falls with a solid thud as I pick my foot up and put it down in a different spot. My feet like the mess—it reminds them they're home.

I slowly get dressed, turn the silver handle to let myself inside, and am immediately greeted with the warmth of a fire. His space is lit with mellow antique lamps and votive candles. I smell mulled wine and can hear light instrumental music playing in the corner of the room. And then I spot Vulnerability—his shaggy, curly blond hair falls past his ears, just above his shoulders, and when his seafoam eyes spot me, he smiles with his whole body. My stomach drops in motion with the waves outside. Vulnerability is my aphrodisiac.

We sit and talk for hours, well into the night. We flirt with a hand on the forearm or a coy smile. We laugh out loud, uninhibited. We talk about heartbreak and rejection in an intimate tone, revealing scars and lessons that we carry with us. Intimacy with Vulnerability is what keeps me feeling alive. When I'm with him, I feel seen, which can feel scary. I feel raw, but at peace. I'm held by the care in his voice and by his eyes, which a thousand ships before have ventured across, knowing that it was

Vulnerability or bust—understanding that the chance to connect with him meant coming home. And that even if the ship were to sink, there would be no home to return to without him.

The moon is still out when I head back, but barely. The sun is now making her grand entry as I walk carefully down the terra-cotta path back toward the beach, catching the last silver notes of the moon in the dusty millers that guide my way.

As I turn to look back once more, I see him washing dishes and whistling ever so slightly to the music that still plays on.

Vulnerability leaves me bare, but it's worth every second of cold air on my skin to feel warmth in my bones.

Inspiration

greet Inspiration with eyes closed.

They touch my face ever so gently—first my eyelids, then my cheeks, moving down to my lips. I smile and grab their hand in mine. Their skin is so soft. It feels welcoming.

Inspiration is a forever lover of mine, but not mine to keep. They move with the wind and the tide. They conspire with the moon. They are quirky and free and intoxicating; my go-to muse and friend.

Their home is a humble blue bungalow that looks white from the sun. Its large-paned windows and French doors let in inviting, warm light. The white walls offer space and stillness. It's here that I meet Inspiration. In the calm. The quiet. It's here that I hear them loudest; their raspy voice and their gentle nudges feel like whispers from the gods themselves.

Before long, the quiet is replaced with an electricity and the feeling of being alive. The plants that hang inside their home talk nonstop. They cheer and clap with their long green arms. "They're back!" they yell. "They're back." I cuddle up with Inspiration and their plants, listening to story after story. Outside, the waves roll spiritedly; inside, their curly red hair bounces when they laugh, and their teeth show coyly when they flirt. My heart leaps, my stomach sinks—I'm hopelessly and madly in love. And it shows.

We walk down to the shore to search for sea glass; light-blue pieces collect in their hands. Light-blue pieces are rare. Light-blue pieces bring out their eyes.

I marvel at how my senses tingle simply from being around them. The world takes on an entirely new perspective, and I find life everywhere; in the lines that make up a shell and the way the water and sun dance over ridges in the sand. They are boundless.

We head back to their cottage, sea glass in tow, and devour their cinnamon rice pudding—a recipe passed down from their great-grandmother.

Our mouths are full of cream and spice, their hand is on mine, and the sun is setting slowly, coating the water with the illusion of a million diamonds.

I think I'll stay a bit longer.

Workbook Pages for
transcendent

STEP 1: GREET

You feel an emotion is present. Say hello and acknowledge that it's here while doing your best not to attach judgment or try to change it, fix it, or remove it. Let it take up space. You can do this. Your body can hold it all.

Now, you can name it. Hello, ... Welcome.

In my body

You feel like . . .

. . . .

. . . .

. . . .

. . . .

. . . .

You taste like . . .

....
....
....
....
....
....

You smell like . . .

....
....
....
....
....
....

You make me want to . . .

....
....
....
....
....
....
....

As a messenger

You teach me . . .

....
....
....
....
....
....

You show me . . .

....
....
....
....
....
....

You need this to feel seen and heard . . .

....
....
....
....
....
....

227

Your secret is . . .

....

....

....

....

....

....

....

IF YOU NEED A RAINCHECK:

You need me to make space for you right now, but I don't have the time, accessibility, or availability at the moment. I have a sweet little sun-filled room where you can sit and wait. I'll be back. In the meantime, know that I see you and I'm here to listen.

Time I'll be back:

....

....

....

....

....

....

....

STEP 2: SIT

Hi, it's me. I'm here and ready to sit down to get to know you better. I know you have messages to share and ways to help me grow and heal. Let's sit together and discover the reason for your visit.

What activating event (an experience or a trigger) has currently introduced me to this emotion?

. . . .

. . . .

. . . .

. . . .

. . . .

. . . .

Right after the activating event and before I found myself with this emotion, there's a voice. This can be a belief or a story—something we tell ourselves either out of conditioning or previous experiences. What does this voice or this story say?

. . . .

. . . .

. . . .

. . . .

. . . .

. . . .

How does this story make me feel?

. . . .

. . . .

. . . .

. . . .

. . . .

. . . .

. . . .

. . . .

. . . .

And how does this emotion cause me to react?

. . . .

. . . .

. . . .

. . . .

. . . .

. . . .

. . . .

. . . .

. . . .

How can I honor exactly how I feel? How can I respect what I need most in this moment?

What is one thing I can do for myself while I'm feeling this emotion that will bring me nourishment? What feels safe here?

STEP 3: CONVERSE

I'm glad we decided to sit down. It may not have been easy or simple, but it created space to understand each other better. It's time for a heart-to-heart.

Time to cue into my senses: Is it cold or warm? Does a breeze blow, or is it humid and thick? What do I feel on my skin when I close my eyes? What do I taste in the air? What smells draw me in? What colors stand out to me?

....

....

....

....

....

....

....

....

....

....

....

....

....

....

Where is our meeting place? Am I at my emotion's home, or do we meet somewhere else? Describe the landscape.

What does their home look like? Is their front door ornate or plain? Explain the exterior of their home and what surrounds it.

When I step inside their house, what textures do I find? What aesthetic themes emerge? Does it feel warm and cozy or minimalistic and drab? Is there food cooking or the scent of flowers on the table? What stands out to me about stepping into their world?

When I see the emotion, what does he/she/they look like? What feels striking about them?

What is their disposition? Are they kind? Jovial? Rugged? Quiet?

....

....

....

....

....

....

....

....

....

Do they have a hobby? What do they love to do? What makes them
come alive?

....

....

....

....

....

....

....

....

....

....

What hurts them, scares them, worries them?

....

....

....

....

....

....

....

....

....

....

What about them surprises me? Speak to their duality.

....

....

....

....

....

....

....

....

....

....

What stories do they share? What past lives do I learn about? What do they need me to know? Write some dialogue.

. . . .

. . . .

. . . .

. . . .

. . . .

. . . .

. . . .

. . . .

. . . .

. . . .

What is one element about our time together that feels important or stands out?

. . . .

. . . .

. . . .

. . . .

. . . .

. . . .

. . . .

. . . .

. . . .

Is there a shifted perspective and/or physical item(s) I walk away with that reminds me of our time together?

. . . .

. . . .

. . . .

. . . .

. . . .

. . . .

. . . .

. . . .

. . . .

What is this emotion here to tell me?

. . . .

. . . .

. . . .

. . . .

. . . .

. . . .

. . . .

. . . .

. . . .

What is one thing I can do right now to help myself and this emotion feel more loved, seen, and accepted?

STEP 4: GRATITUDE AND GOODBYE

I am so grateful for you because you are a part of me. And I am so grateful for me because I am here—growing, committing, and recommitting, messy and disheveled and present. I am a human, and for that I applaud myself. This is my thank-you letter to my emotion and to myself. I acknowledge us for who we are as fully as I can—always holding the easy, the hard, and everything in between.

What insight(s) did I uncover that I'd like to thank my emotion for leading me to?

. . . .

. . . .

. . . .

. . . .

. . . .

. . . .

. . . .

. . . .

. . . .

. . . .

. . . .

. . . .

. . . .

What part of my emotion and myself am I able to shed a softer light on?

....
....
....
....
....
....
....
....
....
....

What newfound gratitude do I have for myself and my emotion?

....
....
....
....
....
....
....
....
....
....
....

What story was I able to reframe about this emotion?

....
....
....
....
....
....
....
....
....
....

How does this new thought/perspective make me feel?

....
....
....
....
....
....
....
....
....
....

When I alchemize/process this emotion, what other supportive emotions do I have access to?

....

....

....

....

....

....

....

....

....

How has this process shifted the way I react/respond to feeling this emotion, whether toward myself or toward someone else?

....

....

....

....

....

....

....

....

....

....

Final Reflections

Gratitudes

This page is one of my favorite parts of writing a book. The deepest thank-you to my family and friends for their emotional and physical support during my writing this book and always. You make being a human easier.

Thank you to my parents for consistently holding my hand and reminding me of myself when I feel scared, doubtful, or altogether tired. Thank you for always believing in me. It's because of you that I feel safe and supported to be vulnerable, to be human, to be me.

Thank you to my husband for being the hurricane ties, the muse, the mirror, and the soft place to rest and restore. Thank you for watching our sweet boy so I can write. Thank you for always encouraging me to be me. And for dancing in the metaphorical and literal mess. This book, our life, would not be without you.

Thank you to my friends for the endless hours of voice memos, for reading my manuscript and giving insight, for stepping into this world with me and for accepting me as I am; you remind me what home feels like, and I'm so grateful for you.

Thank you to my agent, Michelle Tessler, for taking a chance on me from the very beginning. For helping me write the proposal, for believing in its worth, and for leading me to TarcherPerigee. I will be forever grateful for our relationship.

Thank you to my editor, Sara Carder, for your unending kindness, patience, and support. This felt like a divinely orchestrated match from the beginning. *Dwell* would not be what it is without your help and guidance. And to the entire TarcherPerigee team—copyediting, project management, art, design, marketing, PR, and beyond. You helped me bring this to life. Thank you.

And to the reader—thank you for being brave, for showing up when it's heavy and it hurts, and for allowing joy to fill your life. Thank you for being with me in these pages. Being a human is complex and hard and at times dizzying, but you're doing it, and it's been my biggest honor to do so alongside you.

Sources

Adam, Emma K., Louise C. Hawkley, Brigitte M. Kudielka, and John T. Cacioppo. "Day-to-Day Dynamics of Experience—Cortisol Associations in a Population-Based Sample of Older Adults." *Proceedings of the National Academy of Sciences* 103, no. 45 (2006): 17058–63. https://doi.org/10.1073/pnas.0605053103.

Baumeister, R. F., and M. R. Leary. "The Need to Belong: Desire for Interpersonal Attachments as a Fundamental Human Motivation." *Psychological Bulletin* 117, no. 3 (May 1995): 497–529. PMID: 7777651.

Brackett, Marc. *Permission to Feel: Unlocking the Power of Emotions to Help Our Kids, Ourselves, and Our Society Thrive.*

Brown, Brené. *Atlas of the Heart: Mapping Meaningful Connection and the Language of Human Experience.*

Catalino, Lahnna I., Sara B. Algoe, and Barbara L. Fredrickson. "Prioritizing Positivity: An Effective Approach to Pursuing Happiness?" *Emotion* 14, no. 6 (2014): 1155–61. https://doi.org/10.1037/a0038029.

Erochina, Varvara. Be With. https://www.bewith.org.

Estés, Clarissa Pinkola. *Women Who Run with the Wolves: Myths and Stories of the Wild Woman Archetype.*

Hawkley, Louise C., and John T. Cacioppo. "Loneliness and Pathways to Disease." *Brain, Behavior, and Immunity* 17, suppl. no. 1 (February 2003): 98–105. https://doi.org/10.1016/s0889-1591(02)00073-9.

Hawkley, Louise C., Christopher M. Masi, Jarett D. Berry, and John T. Cacioppo.

"Loneliness Is a Unique Predictor of Age-Related Differences in Systolic Blood Pressure." *Psychology and Aging* 21, no. 1 (March 2006): 152–64. https://doi.org/10.1037/0882-7974.21.1.152.

Heinrich, Liesl M., and Eleonora Gullone. "The Clinical Significance of Loneliness: A Literature Review." *Clinical Psychology Review* 26, no. 6 (October 2006): 695–718. https://doi.org/10.1016/j.cpr.2006.04.002.

Over, Harriet. "The Origins of Belonging: Social Motivation in Infants and Young Children." *Philosophical Transactions of the Royal Society B: Biological Sciences* 371, no. 1686 (2016): 20150072. https://doi.org/10.1098/rstb.2015.0072.

Rilke, Rainer Maria. *Letters to a Young Poet.*

Tangney, June P., Roy F. Baumeister, and Angie Luzio Boone. "High Self-Control Predicts Good Adjustment, Less Pathology, Better Grades, and Interpersonal Success." *Journal of Personality* 72, no. 2 (2004): 271–324. https://doi.org/10.1111/j.0022-3506.2004.00263.x.

Zhivotovskaya, Emiliya. The Flourishing Center. 2016. https://theflourishingcenter.com.

Further Reading

Brackett, Marc. *The Permission to Feel: Unlocking the Power of Emotions to Help Our Kids, Ourselves, and Our Society Thrive*. New York: Celadon Books, 2019.

Brown, Brené. *Atlas of the Heart: Mapping Meaningful Connection and the Language of Human Experience*. New York: Random House, 2021.

Cain, Susan. *Bittersweet: How Sorrow and Longing Make Us Whole*. New York: Crown Publishing Group, 2022.

Erochina, Varvara. Be With. https://www.bewith.org.

Estés, Clarissa Pinkola. *Women Who Run with the Wolves: Myths and Stories of the Wild Woman Archetype*. New York: Ballantine Books, 1992.

Glatzel, Mara. *Needy: How to Advocate for Your Needs and Claim Your Sovereignty*. Louisville, CO: Sounds True, 2023.

Olivera, Lisa. *Already Enough: A Path to Self-Acceptance*. New York: Simon & Schuster, 2022.

Rilke, Rainer Maria. *Letters to a Young Poet*. New York: W. W. Norton, 1993.

Photo by Liesl Claire Photography

Devon is an author and storyteller finding inspiration in the human experience. She believes that emotions are messengers—a universal language of humanity that helps connect us to ourselves and others. Outside of writing, Devon makes pottery and spends time with her son, her husband, and their pup (preferably outdoors and preferably somewhere wild).